W9-BUE-460

A BASIC COURSE

IN AMERICAN SIGN LANGUAGE

TOM HUMPHRIES
CAROL PADDEN
TERRENCE J. O'ROURKE

STUDENT STUDY GUIDE

Frances S. DeCapite

T·J·PUBLISHERS

Illustrations by Frank Allen Paul

Cover Design by Eugene Orr

Copyright 1986 by T.J. Publishers, Inc.

Published by T.J. Publishers, Inc.
817 Silver Spring Avenue
Silver Spring, Maryland 20910

First Printing, September 1986
Second Printing, January 1988
Third Printing, October 1988
Fourth Printing, September 1989
Fifth Printing, September 1990
Sixth Printing, October 1991
Seventh Printing, August 1992
Eighth Printing, August 1993
Ninth Printing, May 1994
Tenth Printing, September 1995
Eleventh Printing, September 1996
Twelfth Printing, October 1997

ISBN 0-932666-33-7

TABLE OF CONTENTS

95010

ACKNOWLEDGEMENTS

This book is dedicated to the students of American Sign Language (ASL) at Cuyahoga Community College in Cleveland, Ohio. Their interest in deaf people has made the teaching of sign language a distinct pleasure. This book is a byproduct of their contagious enthusiasm.

The faculty and staff at Cuyahoga Community College deserve a special thanks for their total support of the ASL program. Rae Rohfeld, Rita Gitsen, Evelyn Penza, and Penny Goldstine were most closely involved with the program. The College has proven itself to be a friend of hearing-impaired people and an advocate of their language and culture.

For their encouragement and support, I wish to thank my family and my very special friends: Joe Sosnowski, Lorraine Durkalski, Debbie Kiraly, Pat Etchell, Grace DiBello, and Mary Lou Bertram.

Cleveland Heights, Ohio   Frances S. DeCapite
September 1986

INTRODUCTION

The student study guide was developed for use with the first and second editions of the instructional textbook, **A Basic Course in American Sign Language (ABC-ASL)**. Designed for an indepth understanding of this communication medium, the study guide contains exercises that reinforce the more difficult principles in the ABC-ASL textbook. However, the study guide does not cover every principle in the textbook. In some cases, two or more principles are combined into one exercise in the study guide.

The study guide is based on the format of the ABC-ASL textbook. Each principle or basic sentence structure is presented in appropriate sequence and in the format of a box. Each exercise in the word order of ASL is supplemented by an English translation in appendix III. Several exercises draw material from previous lessons, thereby functioning as a built-in review of the ASL principles under study.

The practice sentences are divided into two separate sets which enable students to work together in pairs. As one student practices expressive skills, the other practices receptive skills, and then they may reverse roles. With ample material for extensive practice, the exercises enable students to generate their own sentences and short stories and to apply the principles of ASL in the process.

Students are able to develop effective signing habits through the exclusive use of signed vocabulary. Illustrations of signs were selected on the basis of their difficulty and were published without captions along the margins of the sets. As a result, this format provides students with visual clues to difficult signs used in the practice sentences.

Many signing exercises also emphasize the importance of using appropriate facial expressions. Mime, a natural and integral part of ASL, is commonly used by the hearing-impaired. Many hearing individuals consider the use of this communication mode as an awkward experience and require practice in this unfamiliar area.

The initial reaction of beginning sign language students is to fingerspell words for which they do not know the signs, thus forming a habit that is difficult to unlearn. Students are more inclined to fingerspell than to select a better alternative, i.e. gesturing, miming, or using a sign that has a similar meaning. This guide will help students to overcome this fingerspelling habit.

The study guide contains four appendices. The first appendix is a list of numbers to help students develop expressive and receptive numerical mastery in their everyday discourse. The second appendix consists of interesting and innovative suggestions for mime activities. The third appendix provides the answer key for the ASL/English translations. The fourth appendix consists of the manual alphabet and numerical illustrations.

Students will find this study guide to be extremely helpful in their quest to attain mastery of American Sign Language.

NOTES TO THE INSTRUCTOR

These exercises serve as a supplement to the lessons in **A Basic Course in American Sign Language.** The practice material will be invaluable to the student striving for a higher level of signing skill and for mastery of the subtleties of American Sign Language (ASL). The flexible arrangement of lessons makes the guide practical for use both in the classroom and in laboratory settings.

The practice sentences are divided into two sets which enable the students to work in pairs. This strategy frees the instructor to move about the classroom, attend to the individual needs of students, and reinforce the learning process by providing feedback in the areas of sign formation, body movement, facial expression, and sentence structure.

This practice material may also be used for further positive reinforcement:

1. As homework.

2. As a basis for the students to construct their own sentences while working in pairs. For instance, a student may sign a practice sentence and the partner may generate feedback, perhaps by asking questions based on the topic under discussion.

3. As additional examples to reinforce the concepts being introduced.

4. As a valid measurement of the expressive and receptive skills of the students.

5. As review or evaluation opportunities for each section.

The guide provides more than 75 exercises upon which the students may improvise their own sentences or short paragraphs. These exercises enable the instructor to assess the mastery of ASL principles exhibited by individual students. A student's response will indicate the need for additional review or practice.

The individual exercise sets may also reinforce learning material used to supplement the lessons in the text. These exercises will encourage students to practice signed sentences of their own creation. This practice may be assigned as homework or for eventual class presentation. Another instructional strategy would be to present the material to the whole class and to encourage the class to plan its response within a few minutes. This presentation may be managed in a variety of ways. These flexible approaches are useful in terms of practice activity.

The study guide provides many interesting and innovative suggestions for mime activities. Mime is a natural and integral part of ASL. Many hearing individuals find this communication mode to be awkward, therefore these miming activities are designed to encourage practice in this unfamiliar area of communication. Students will find this text helpful in their quest to master American Sign Language.

The guide includes a reference section with up-to-date information on current resources for instructors. In addition, the guide contains an annotated listing of videotapes to supplement the instructional exercises.

Instructors who have used the guide's instructional strategies verify that they dramatically reduced the amount of time required to attain fluency in ASL. Thus, the systematic practice required to master basic sign vocabulary and ASL sentence structures has been a proven approach. In the majority of instances, the end result has been that students develop confidence in their ability to communicate effectively with the hearing impaired.

NOTES TO THE STUDENT

The student study guide is designed to effectively reinforce each new concept presented in **A Basic Course in American Sign Language(ABC-ASL).** In order to attain a complete mastery of the linguistic structure and vocabulary of American Sign Language (ASL), the student must focus on a single concept before moving on to subsequent concepts. The validity of this learning approach is based on teaching experience and empirical research.

The guide provides extensive exercises for most lessons in the text. The practice sentences are constructed in the word order of ASL. The material places the emphasis on new sign vocabulary and sentence structures, in addition to the reinforcement of previous learning. It encourages the student to develop an important capability, i.e. to improvise ASL sentences. It is suggested that when the student signs his own sentences, he should analyze all the structures learned to that point. It is difficult to recall sentence structures that differ from sentence structures used in English. Consequently, the student may sign as closely as possible to the English word order. In order to avoid this tenacious habit, the student should practice a variety of unfamiliar ASL sentence structures.

The guide stresses the importance of facial expression and body movement as appropriate adjuncts of ASL. The student is reminded that a hearing-impaired individual obtains most of his information visually, thus the need to incorporate these critical elements into the sign communication process. Signing without facial expression can be most boring to watch and can result in a misunderstanding or at least a failure to communicate. Even in instances of simple sentences, the student should develop the ability to accompany each signed sentence with the appropriate facial expressions. For example, the student may sign "I ANGRY!" with a blank expression, with the result that one's feelings are not adequately expressed to a hearing-impaired individual. As a further example, the type of facial expression used with short sentence, "SHE BEAUTIFUL!", can convey an infinite variety of meanings—admiration, jealousy, surprise, "longing to be near her", and so forth.

Many first-time ASL students recognize that the simultaneous use of signs, facial expressions, and body movements may be difficult. If this is a problem for the student, it is suggested that the student practice basic signs as a first step. With the signs fully mastered, the student will be free to focus on the critical nonverbal behaviors in ASL sentence structures.

Directional Symbols

This text uses the following directional symbols:

1. (right), (left)

   When either of these symbols is used, the sign should be executed in that structural sequence or location.

   Example: New York (right) L.A. (left)

   The sign "New York" should be made to the right; the sign "L.A." should be made to the left.

2. (point right), (point left)

   When either of these symbols is used, the signer should point as indicated to the right or to the left after the sign has been executed.

   Example: Restaurant (point right)

   After signing "restaurant", the signer should point to the right.

Basic Sentence Structure: Sentences With Predicate Adjectives

It is common in simple sentences to repeat the subject pronoun at the end of the sentence.

■ SET I
Practice Sentences

1. JOHN STRONG.

2. KATHY ANGRY.

3. YOU SHORT, YOU.

4. PRETTY, YOU (plural).

5. YOU INTERESTING YOU.

6. BEAUTIFUL SHE.

7. JACKIE DEAF.

8. THEY TIRED THEY.

9. JENNIFER MAD.

10. PAULA HARD-OF-HEARING.

■ *NOTES*

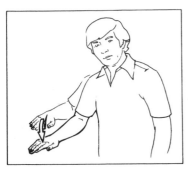

Basic Sentence Structure: Sentences With Predicate Adjectives

It is common in simple sentences to repeat the subject pronoun at the end of the sentence.

■ **SET II**

Practice Sentences

1. I HARD-OF-HEARING I.

2. PAUL TIRED.

3. LINDA DUMB.

4. LOIS SLEEPY.

5. I DEAF I.

6. YOU (plural) PRETTY, YOU (plural).

7. BOBBY STRONG.

8. HAPPY THEY.

9. YOU (plural) SHORT.

10. THEY HEARING.

■ *NOTES*

■ **EXERCISE 1**

Sign a sentence . . .

1. which includes the sign *"HEARING"*.

2. which includes the sign *"SAD"* with an appropriate facial expression.

3. which includes the sign *"BIG"*.

4. which includes the sign *"ANGRY"* with an appropriate facial expression.

5. which includes the sign *"STRONG"*.

6. which includes the sign *"TIRED"* with an appropriate facial expression.

7. with a disgusted facial expression which includes the sign *"UGLY"*.

8. with an angry facial expression which includes the sign *"I"*.

4

■ *NOTES*

■LESSON 2

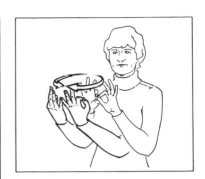

Basic Sentence Structure: Sentences With Identifying Nouns and Using Two Third-Person Pronouns

When the sentence refers to two different persons such as HE and SHE, or HE and HE (meaning another person), point to two different locations for the different persons. Remember that if the persons are not present, the signer can refer to one person on one side of the signer and the other person on the opposite side.

■ SET I
Practice Sentences

1. SHE, HER MOTHER. (Use two people in the classroom)

2. SHE, HER FRIEND. (Use two people in the classroom)

3. SHE, HER NIECE. (Use two people in the classroom)

4. HE, HER STUDENT. (Use two people in the classroom)

5. YOUR TEACHER (point right) MAN. HE, MY GRANDFATHER.

6. JOHN (point right) HARD-OF-HEARING. JUDY (point left) DEAF. HE, HER TEACHER.

7. LOUIE (point right) MY FRIEND. PAT (point left) HIS UNCLE. HE (Pat) HIS TEACHER. HE (Pat) SMART. HE (Louie) DUMB.

8. MY STUDENT LORI (point right) DEAF. SHE PRETTY. MY STUDENT GLORIA (point left) DEAF. SHE UGLY. SHE (Lori) HER AUNT.

Basic Sentence Structure: Sentences With Identifying Nouns and Using Two Third-Person Pronouns

When the sentence refers to two different persons such as HE and SHE, or HE and HE (meaning another person), point to two different locations for the different persons. Remember that if the persons are not present, the signer can refer to the person on one side of the signer and the other person on the opposite side.

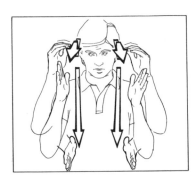

■ SET II

Practice Sentences

1. HE, HER FATHER. (Use two people in the classroom)

2. SHE, HER GRANDMOTHER. (Use two people in the classroom)

3. SHE, HER TEACHER. (Use two people in the classroom)

4. SHE, HIS AUNT. (Use two people in the classroom)

5. LISA (point right) DEAF. HER GRANDFATHER HEARING. HER GRANDMOTHER HARD-OF-HEARING. HER PARENTS DEAF.

6. PAULA (point right) MY FRIEND. HER FRIEND KATHY (point left) PRETTY. SHE (Kathy) HARD-OF-HEARING.

7. MY AUNT (point right) DEAF. SHE TEACHER. MY FRIEND FRANK (point left) HER STUDENT. HE HEARING.

8. MY MOTHER (point right) SHORT. MY FATHER (point left) TALL. I SHORT. SHE (my mother) DEAF. HE (my father) HARD-OF-HEARING. I DEAF.

■ EXERCISE I

Sign a sentence . . .

1. in which you identify a person as *"MY GOOD-FRIEND"*.

2. with a proud facial expression which includes the sign *"HUSBAND"*.

3. in which you identify a person as an American.

4. which includes the sign *"CHILD"*.

5. which includes the sign *"WEAK"*.

6. with a mocking facial expression which includes the sign *"SHORT"*.

7. which includes the sign *"DUMB"*.

■ EXERCISE II

Complete the following sentences:

1. JACK MY GOOD-FRIEND.
   HE _____ .

2. MY MOTHER PRETTY.
   SHE _____ .

3. YOUR DAUGHTER SHORT.
   SHE _____ .

4. MY BROTHER SMART.
   HE _____ .

5. MY TEACHER INTERESTING.
   SHE _____ .

8

■ *NOTES*

LESSON 3

Basic Sentence Structure: Pronouns and Nouns

Pronouns are often used together with nouns. In these cases, the pronoun functions like the English word, *the*. The pronoun can occur either before or after the noun.

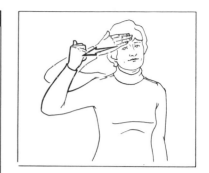

■ SET I
Practice Sentences

1. GIRL, SHE LIKE ME.

2. MY FATHER, HE COOK + AGENT.

3. JOHN, HE KNOW MY SISTER.

4. MY UNCLE, HE KNOW YOUR NAME.

5. YOUR FATHER, HE REMEMBER MY MOTHER.

6. PAULA, SHE FORGET PAPER.

7. YOUR MOTHER, SHE LOSE BOOK.

8. MY WIFE, SHE HAVE PAPER.

9. MY HUSBAND, HE NEED CAR.

10. MY AUNT, SHE TEACHER.

■ *NOTES*

Basic Sentence Structure: Pronouns and Nouns

Pronouns are often used together with nouns. In these cases, the pronoun functions like the English word, *the.* The pronoun can occur either before or after the noun.

■ SET II
Practice Sentences

1. YOUR TEACHER, SHE WANT BOOK.

2. MY AUNT, SHE WANT MONEY.

3. HIS WIFE, SHE STUDENT.

4. MY DAUGHTER, SHE PRACTICE SIGN.

5. MY BROTHER, HE LIKE CAR.

6. YOUR MOTHER, SHE REMEMBER MY CAR.

7. WOMAN, SHE NEED CHAIR.

8. MY FRIEND, HE NEED CAR.

9. MY STUDENT, SHE HAVE PAPER.

10. MY FRIEND, SHE DANCE + AGENT.

■ *NOTES*

Basic Sentence Structure: Adjectives and Nouns

Adjectives appear either before or after the noun.

■ SET I

Practice Sentences

1. PAUL, HE LIKE PRETTY WOMAN.

2. MOTHER, SHE WANT PAPER BLUE.

3. I HAVE BED NEW.

4. I KNOW SHORT WOMAN.

5. HIS SISTER LOSE BOX RED.

6. I HAVE HOUSE NEW.

7. MY NIECE, SHE LIKE CAR BLUE.

8. I NEED PRACTICE NEW SIGN.

9. I KNOW OLD MAN.

10. I FIND CHAIR BLACK.

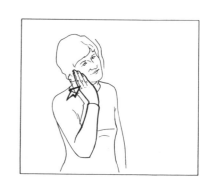

■ *NOTES*

Basic Sentence Structure: Adjectives and Nouns

Adjectives appear either before or after the noun.

■ SET II

Practice Sentences

1. LOUIE, HE FIND ORANGE BOOK.

2. I WANT TALK-WITH MAN OLD.

3. MY CLASS WANT BOOK NEW.

4. MY MOTHER, SHE HAVE YELLOW CHAIR.

5. I ENJOY LEARN NEW SIGN.

6. I REMEMBER OLD WOMAN.

7. MY BROTHER, HE HAVE PAPER GREEN.

8. JACK, HE FIND PACKAGE WHITE.

9. YOUR GRANDMOTHER HAVE DESK BEAUTIFUL.

10. I LIKE NEW BOOK.

■ *NOTES*

■ EXERCISE I

Sign a sentence . . .

1. with an angry facial expression using the sign *"FORGET"*.

2. which starts, *"MY MOTHER, SHE . . ."*.

3. using the sign *"SHE"* to refer to someone who is not present.

4. with an excited facial expression using the sign *"OUR"*.

5. using the signs *"HE"* and *"SHE"* to refer to two people who are not present.

6. with a disappointed facial expression using the sign *"LOSE"*.

7. in which you identify a person as *"MY FRIEND"*.

8. using the classifier *"C1:L̈L̈"*.

9. with a pleased facial expression using the sign *"ENJOY"*.

10. using the signs *"HE"* and *"SHE"* to refer to your *"BROTHER"* and *"MOTHER"* who are not present.

11. with a determined facial expression using the sign *"NEED"*.

12. in which the adjective follows the noun.

13. in which you identify a person as *"MY GRANDMOTHER"*.

14. in which you use the suffix *"AGENT"*.

15. in which the adjective precedes the noun.

■■■ **LESSON 3**

Exercises

■ **EXERCISE II**

Sign the following numbers exactly as you would say them:

SET A.

3	75	230	611,325
7	13	7,498	944,736
25	723	6,903	729,897
76	540	3,690	853,467
97	788	9,888	690,886
29	994	7,278	433,476
57	321	99,132	10,216,118
87	527	13,245	5,390,462
28	211	21,367	1,779,321
57	110	14,986	12,442,242

SET B.

8	86	750	789,875
11	92	5,143	832,148
14	198	6,897	278,450
16	357	8,809	193,460
48	960	9,859	224,698
23	546	6,658	3,473,790
41	709	89,706	13,645,398
36	758	24,755	25,478,900
37	175	15,253	8,687,008
6	389	17,183	142,365,615

Exercises

■ EXERCISE III

Sign the following set of sentences with the facial expression given in the parentheses. Using your voice, without signing, ask your partner the questions that follow the selection. Your partner should *sign* the answers related to the information presented and *speak* the answers on how you feel about that information.

MY FATHER, HE SHORT.   (Disgusted)
MY UNCLE, HE TALL.   (Wishful)
I SHORT I.   (Disgusted)

    1. Who is tall in this story?
    2. How do I feel about being short?

2. MY FRIEND RITA WANT TABLE ORANGE!   (Incredulous)

    1. What does my friend want?
    2. What is my friend's name?
    3. How do I feel about her choice?

3. MY NIECE, SHE PRETTY.   (Pleasant)
   HER MOTHER, SHE PRETTY.   (Pleasant)
   SHE (her mother), MY SISTER,   (Proud)
   SHE.

    1. Who is pretty in this story?
    2. How do I feel about my sister?

4. JOHN FORGET HIS BLUE BOOK.   (Shocked and upset)

    1. Who forgot his book?
    2. How do I feel about John forgetting his book?

16

■ *NOTES*

LESSON 4

Negatives

There are several ways to form negative sentences. All are accompanied by a negative marker, ____ n ____ , which is:
1. a headshake
2. eyebrows squeezed together

The different forms of negative sentences are:
1. Use of NOT. NOT either comes before the verb or at the end of the sentence.
2. Use of Negative Incorporation. The negative of these verbs, KNOW, WANT, and LIKE, are formed by incorporating an outward, twisting movement.
3. Use of Negative Marker. ____ n ____ may be used alone to negate a simple sentence.

■ SET I
Practice Sentences

In sentences 1–4, add the sign "NOT" or a negative incorporation to make the sentences negative.

1. JOHN WANT PAPER BLUE.

2. JEAN, SHE WANT TABLE NEW.

3. SHE, MY SISTER.

4. I LIKE FINGERSPELLING.

In sentences 5–8, make the sentences negative using only the negative marker.

5. I SURPRISED I.

6. LISA, SHE UNDERSTAND MOVIE.

7. CAT EXPENSIVE.

8 FOOD TASTE GOOD.

Negatives

There are several ways to form negative sentences. All are accompanied by a negative marker, ___ n ___ , which is:
1. a headshake
2. eyebrows squeezed together

The different forms of negative sentences are:
1. Use of NOT. NOT either comes before the verb or at the end of the sentence.
2. Use of Negative Incorporation. The negative of these verbs, KNOW, WANT, and LIKE, are formed by incorporating an outward, twisting movement.
3. Use of Negative Marker. ___ n ___ may be used alone to negate a simple sentence.

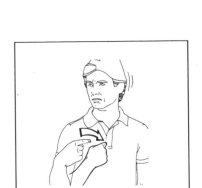

■ SET II
Practice Sentences

In sentences 1–4, add the sign "NOT" or a negative incorporation to make the sentences negative.

1. I SEE YOUR TEACHER.

2. MRS. SMITH, SHE MY AUNT.

3. I LIKE PRACTICE.

4. SHE WANT TABLE YELLOW.

In sentences 5–8, make the sentences negative using only the negative marker.

5. JACK LOSE PAPER.

6. FRAN, SHE AMERICAN.

7. JOAN, SHE SHORT.

8. SENTENCE WRONG.

Responses to Yes/No Questions

Affirmative Responses to Yes/No Questions and Negative Questions

When responding affirmatively to Yes/No Questions and Negative Questions, a positive nod of the head accompanies the positive response. The YES sign may be dropped from the response.

■ SET I

Practice Sentences

Tell your partner to answer the following questions in the affirmative.

$$\overline{q}$$
1. YOU LEARN VOCABULARY YOU?

$$\overline{q}$$
2. DESK WHITE?

$$\overline{q}$$
3. YOU PREFER CAR HEAVY?

$$\overline{q}$$
4. YOU NEED BOOK NEW?

$$\overline{q}$$
5. BOOK INTERESTING?

$$\overline{nq}$$
6. TABLE NOT HEAVY?

$$\overline{nq}$$
7. YOU NOT ENJOY READ YOU?

$$\overline{nq}$$
8. YOUR FATHER NOT HEARING?

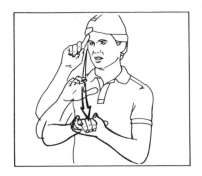

Affirmative Responses to Yes/No Questions and Negative Questions

When responding affirmatively to Yes/No Questions and Negative Questions, a positive nod of the head accompanies the positive response. The YES sign may be dropped from the response.

■ SET II

Practice Sentences

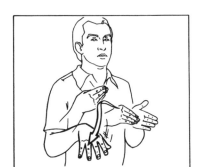

Tell your partner to answer the following questions in the affirmative.

$$\overline{\text{q}}$$
1. YOU ENJOY CLASS YOU?

$$\overline{\text{q}}$$
2. YOU BELIEVE ME YOU?

$$\overline{\text{q}}$$
3. YOUR GOOD-FRIEND SICK?

$$\overline{\text{q}}$$
4. YOU NEED BOX SMALL?

$$\overline{\text{q}}$$
5. CAR EXPENSIVE?

$$\overline{\text{nq}}$$
6. YOU NOT LOVE ME?

$$\overline{\text{nq}}$$
7. SHE DON'T-WANT ORANGE SHE?

$$\overline{\text{nq}}$$
8. YOU NOT READ EXERCISE 5?

Responses to Negative Questions

Negative Responses to Yes/No Questions and Negative Questions

When responding negatively to Yes/No Questions and Negative Questions, the negative marker accompanies the negative response. The NO sign may be dropped from the response.

■ SET I
Practice Sentences

Tell your partner to answer the following questions negatively.

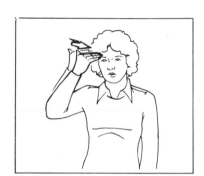

<u>   q   </u>
1. HIS GRANDMOTHER LIKE CAT?

<u>   q   </u>
2. YOUR HOUSE OLD?

<u>   q   </u>
3. YOU KNOW WOMAN MARCIE SMITH YOU?

<u>   q   </u>
4. YOUR AUNT EAT YOUR ORANGE?

<u>   q   </u>
5. SHE NEED PAPER BLUE SHE?

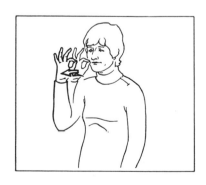

<u>   nq   </u>
6. YOU DON'T-LIKE COOK?

<u>   nq   </u>
7. YOU NOT ANGRY?

Negative Responses to Yes/No Questions and Negative Questions

When responding negatively to Yes/No Questions and Negative Questions, the negative marker accompanies the negative response. The NO sign may be dropped from the response.

■ SET II
Practice Sentences

Tell your partner to answer the following questions negatively.

$$\overline{}\overset{\text{q}}{}$$
1. YOUR PARENTS LIKE DOG?

$$\overline{}\overset{\text{q}}{}$$
2. YOU UNDERSTAND LESSON YOU?

$$\overline{}\overset{\text{q}}{}$$
3. YOU REMEMBER MOVIE NAME YOU?

$$\overline{}\overset{\text{q}}{}$$
4. YOUR NIECE ENJOY DANCE?

$$\overline{}\overset{\text{q}}{}$$
5. YOUR FAMILY LIKE YOUR HUSBAND?

$$\overline{}\overset{\text{nq}}{}$$
6. YOUR TABLE NOT NEW?

$$\overline{}\overset{\text{nq}}{}$$
7. HE DON'T-WANT TEACH HE?

■ NOTES

Exercises

■ EXERCISE I

Sign a sentence . . .

1. which includes the sign *"NOT"*.

2. which you make negative without using the sign *"NOT"*.

3. which uses the sign *"GREEN"* as an adjective which follows the noun.

4. which in English would start, *"ARE YOU . . . ?"*.

5. with a bored facial expression.

6. which in English would start, *"DIDN'T YOU . . . ?"*.

7. which in English would start, *"IS . . . ?"*.

8. with a facial expression seeming to smother laughter which includes the sign *"FORGET"*.

9. which starts, *"MY GRANDFATHER, HE . . . "*.

10. which in English would start, *"DOES . . . ?"*.

11. in which you refer to a person who is not present as *"YOUR NEPHEW"*.

12. which includes the sign *"WHITE-PERSON"*.

13. which in English would start, *"ISN'T . . . ?"*.

14. which includes the sign *"DON'T-KNOW"*.

■ EXERCISE II

Pick three students in the class to sign Dialogue I on page 45 of *A Basic Course in American Sign Language.* To test comprehension, ask the class to answer the following questions:

1. Who is Tom's friend?

2. Where is Jack from?

3. Whom do both Betty and Jack know?

4. What relationship to Bob is Jack?

5. What is Tom's last comment?

■ EXERCISE III

Ask your partner a yes/no question (or a negative yes/no question) about something s/he . . . . Have your partner respond to your questions.

$$\overline{\qquad\qquad \overset{q}{\qquad}\qquad \overset{\_\_}{\qquad}}$$
Example: forget   YOU FORGET BOOK?

1. likes	11. doesn't want
2. needs	12. remembers
3. doesn't remember	13. doesn't need
4. has	14. doesn't know
5. doesn't understand	15. enjoys
6. wants	16. knows
7. found	17. understands
8. doesn't like	18. believes
9. doesn't enjoy	19. doesn't have
10. doesn't believe	20. lost

LESSON 5

Basic Sentence Structure:
Present, Past, Future, and Using FINISH

It is also possible to use FINISH to show that an action has been completed. FINISH appears either before or after the verb.

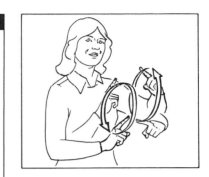

■ SET I

Practice Sentences

1. LONG-TIME-AGO HE LIKE WORK. $\overline{\text{NOW, DON'T-LIKE.}}^{\text{n}}$

2. YESTERDAY COLD.

3. $\overline{\text{THEY FINISH FIND BOX SMALL?}}^{\text{q}}$

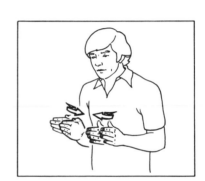

4. TOMORROW SISTER BUY COOKIE.

5. FUTURE I VISIT WASHINGTON.

6. LATER I PRACTICE SIGN.

7. $\overline{\text{SARAH FINISH BUY TTY?}}^{\text{q}}$

8. USED-TO PRACTICE SIGN LANGUAGE. $\overline{\text{NOW, NOT.}}^{\text{n}}$

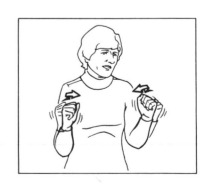

9. JOHN FINISH TO-TELEPHONE JACK.

10. I FINISH WRITE LETTER.

■ NOTES

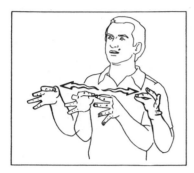

Basic Sentence Structure:
Present, Past, Future, and Using FINISH

It is also possible to use FINISH to show that an action has been completed. FINISH appears either before or after the verb.

■ SET II

Practice Sentences

1. YESTERDAY MY BROTHER FEEL SICK. TODAY IMPROVE.

2. RECENTLY I GO-AWAY WASHINGTON.

3. YESTERDAY NIGHT GRANDMOTHER DIE.

4. FUTURE I BUY CAR NEW.

5. RECENTLY MY SISTER, SHE FIND DOG.

6. I FINISH WRITE SENTENCE.

7. LATER I BUY PAPER.

8. PAUL BUY FINISH BOOK.

9. YESTERDAY I REMEMBER YOUR NAME.

$$\overline{\text{NOW NOT REMEMBER.}}^{\text{n}}$$

10. WORK FINISH.

■ *NOTES*

Exercises

■ EXERCISE I

Sign a sentence . . .

1. in the past tense which includes the sign *"RECENTLY"*.

2. which in English would start, *"AREN'T. . . ?"*.

3. in the past tense using the sign *"FINISH"* to show that the action has been completed and which includes the sign *"HOMEWORK"*.

4. in the future tense which includes the sign *"RESIDENTIAL-SCHOOL"*.

5. which you make negative without using the sign *"NOT"*.

6. with a "cool" facial expression which includes the sign *"NEW"*.

7. with a friendly facial expression which includes the sign *"AUNT"*.

8. in which the adjective precedes the noun.

9. with a nervous facial expression in which you refer to someone who is not present.

10. in which you ask a negative yes/no question.

11. with a reluctant facial expression which includes the sign *"DON'T-LIKE"*.

12. which includes the sign *"NOT"*.

■ EXERCISE II

Sign three sentences about something that has happened to you in the past or will happen to you in the future.

1. _____

2. _____

3. _____

■ EXERCISE III

Sign the following short paragraph. Using your voice and without signing, ask your partner the questions that follow the selection. Your partner should sign the answer back to you.

TOMORROW I GO-AWAY MOVIE NAME "AMERICA".
YESTERDAY SEE MOVIE ABOUT WASHINGTON, D.C. I ENJOY.
 ___n___
INTERESTING. I REMEMBER NAME.
_____ ___q___ _____ ___q___
YOU SEE MOVIE ABOUT WASHINGTON, D.C.? YOU LIKE?
_____ ___q___ _____
YOU REMEMBER NAME?

1. When will I go to the movies?

2. What is the name of the movie that I am going to see?

3. About what was the movie that I saw yesterday?

4. Did I like it?

5. What couldn't I remember about it?

6. What were two of the questions I asked you?

LESSON 6

Basic Sentence Structure:
Object + Subject + Verb

Another common sentence structure is: Object +
Subject + Verb.

■ SET I
Practice Sentences

$$\overline{\quad t \quad}$$
1. MOVIE, MY SISTER SEE FINISH.

$$\overline{\quad t \quad}$$
2. SIGN, I PRACTICE.

$$\overline{\quad t \quad}$$
3. CAR, MY FAMILY NEED.

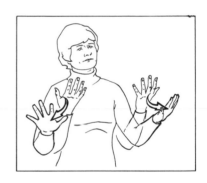

$$\overline{\qquad t \qquad} \ \overline{\qquad n \qquad}$$
4. SCHOOL HEARING, MY FRIEND DEAF DON'T-LIKE.

$$\overline{\ t \ } \ \overline{\quad q \quad}$$
5. READ, YOUR UNCLE ENJOY?

$$\overline{\quad t \quad} \ \overline{\quad n \quad}$$
6. PANTS GREEN, MY SON DON'T-LIKE.

$$\overline{\quad t \quad}$$
7. UMBRELLA, MY FRIEND KATHY NEED.

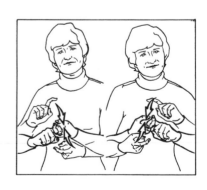

$$\overline{\quad t \quad}$$
8. MY BOOK, TEACHER LOSE.

$$\overline{\quad t \quad}$$
9. MONEY, MY SISTER WANT.

$$\overline{\ t \ } \ \overline{\qquad q \qquad}$$
10. BICYCLE, YOUR DAUGHTER FINISH BUY?

Basic Sentence Structure: Object + Subject + Verb

Another common sentence structure is: Object + Subject + Verb.

■ SET II
Practice Sentences

      t
1. DANCE, I LÍKE.

         t   n
2. SIGN LANGUAGE, MY MOTHER DON'T-KNOW.

      t
3. WASHINGTON, I VISIT FINISH.

      t
4. MY BICYCLE, PAUL, HIS DAUGHTER LOSE.

    t
5. LETTER, I FINISH WRITE.

       t
6. WRIST-WATCH NEW, MY SISTER BUY.

    t
7. UMBRELLA, MY AUNT WANT.

      t
8. GRANDFATHER, SALLY VISIT FINISH.

   t
9. BOOK, I FINISH READ.

   t   n
10. MOVIE, I DON'T-LIKE.

Directional and Non-Directional Verbs

___

Basic Sentence Structure: Directional and Non-Directional Verbs

Some verbs change their movement to indicate the subject and object of the verb—they incorporate the locations of the subject and object pronouns. These verbs are called directional verbs.

■ SET I
Practice Sentences

1. <u>   t   </u>
   MY PICTURE, YESTERDAY I I-SHOW-HER MOTHER. SHE SAY PRETTY.

2. I SHY. YOU YOU-ASK-HER.

3. <u>   t   </u> <u>   q   </u>
   ORANGE, YOU YOU-GIVE-ME, PLEASE?

4. <u>   t   </u> <u>   q   </u>
   MONEY, YOU YOU-GIVE-ME FINISH?

5. <u>   q   </u>
   YOU YOU-ASK-HER BUY ME BOOK NEW?

6. TEACHER SHE-ASK-ME ME;
   <u>   n   </u>
   SHE NOT SHE-ASK-YOU YOU!

7. PAULY, HE HE-TELL-ME J-O-K-E FUNNY.

8. I I-PAY-YOU FINISH!

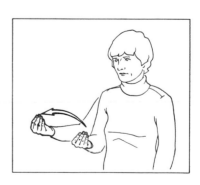

9. SHE SHE-GIVE-CI:C-HER PLANT NAME S-P-I-D-E-R PLANT YESTERDAY.

10. <u>   t   </u> <u>   q   </u>
    PICTURE, YOU FINISH YOU-GIVE-CI:C↑-HER?

▰ LESSON 6

Directional and Non-Directional Verbs

Basic Sentence Structure: Directional and Non-Directional Verbs

Some verbs change their movement to indicate the subject and object of the verb—they incorporate the locations of the subject and object pronouns. These verbs are called directional verbs.

▪ SET II

Practice Sentences

```
            t                q
```
1. YOUR ADDRESS, YOU YOU-TELL-ME FINISH?

```
   t                q
```
2. TTY, I I-GIVE-CI:C↑-YOU FINISH?

```
                               n
```
3. I DON'T-WANT MOTHER SHE-FORCE-ME LEARN DRIVE.

4. MY BROTHER, HE HE-INFLUENCE-ME.

```
   t          t
```
5. JOHN (right), KAREN (left) GOOD-FRIEND. SHE SHE-GIVE-HIM CAT CUTE BEFORE THURSDAY.

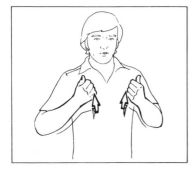

6. BEFORE FRIDAY CONNIE SHE SHE-PAY-ME.
```
                  q
```
BEFORE SATURDAY YOU YOU-PAY-ME?

```
        t
```
7. UMBRELLA NEW, I WANT I-SHOW-YOU.

```
       t                  q
```
8. MY PICTURE, BEFORE MONDAY I I-SEND-YOU?

```
   t         q
```
9. BOOK, YOU YOU-GIVE-CL:C↑-HER FINISH?

```
   t
```
10. WATER, LATER SHE SHE-GIVE-CI:C-YOU.

■ EXERCISE I

Sign two sentences. . . .

1. with an irritated facial expression in which one sentence includes the sign *"DON'T-KNOW"*.

2. with a joyful facial expression in which one sentence includes the sign *"SHE-PAY-ME"*.

3. in the past tense in which the first sentence includes the sign *"FINISH"*.

4. in which one sentence includes the sign *"WRIST-WATCH"* as the object in the *"OBJECT + SUBJECT + VERB"* word order.

5. in the future tense in which one sentence includes the sign *"GO-AWAY"*.

6. in the present tense in which one sentence includes the sign *"YOU-SEND-ME"*.

7. with a nervous facial expression in which one sentence includes the sign *"DOCTOR"* as the object in the *"OBJECT + SUBJECT + VERB"* word order.

8. in the future tense in which one sentence includes the signs *"JOE, HE HE-TELL-YOU"*.

9. in which one sentence includes the sign *"NOT"* at the end of the sentence.

10. in the past tense with a lively facial expression in which the first sentence includes the sign *"FINISH"*.

11. in the past tense in which one sentence includes the sign *"TV"* as the object in the *"OBJECT + SUBJECT + VERB"* word order.

12. in which one sentence is made negative without using the sign *"NOT"*.

■ LESSON 6

Exercises

13. in which the signs "DON'T-WANT" and "LOSE" are included at least once.

14. with a frustrated facial expression in which one sentence includes the sign "I-GIVE-YOU".

15. in which one sentence includes the sign "YOU-ASK-ME".

■ EXERCISE II

Have your partner respond as you ask him/her a yes/no question . . .

1. in the past tense with a contented facial expression using the signs "BEFORE" and "CHEAP".

2. in the future tense using the signs "TOMORROW" and "SCHOOL".

3. in the past tense with a proud facial expression using the signs "RECENTLY" and "BUY".

4. in the future tense in which you identify someone as "MY TEACHER".

5. using the "OBJECT + SUBJECT + VERB" word order.

Have your partner respond as you ask him/her a negative yes/no question . . .

1. in the past tense with a surprised facial expression using the sign "MORNING".

2. in the present tense using the sign "HAPPY" as the predicate adjective.

3. in the future tense with an adjective following a noun.

4. using the sign "YOU-SEND-HER".

5. starting, "MY NIECE, SHE . . ."

6. using the sign "UMBRELLA" as the object in the "OBJECT + SUBJECT + VERB" word order.

■ EXERCISE III

Complete the following sentences:

        $\overline{t}$
1. BREAD,

            $\overline{t}$
2. TELETYPEWRITER,

           $\overline{t}$
3. WRIST-WATCH NEW,

        $\overline{t}$
4. PLANT,

          $\overline{t}$
5. CLOTHES DIRTY,

         $\overline{t}$
6. PANTS BLUE,

         $\overline{t}$
7. BLACK CAT,

        $\overline{t}$
8. WINTER,

        $\overline{t}$
9. BOTTLE,

          $\overline{t}$
10. SCHOOL HEARING,

         $\overline{t}$
11. WASHINGTON,

■ *NOTES*

12. $\overline{\quad \text{t} \quad}$ WATER,

13. $\overline{\qquad\qquad \text{t} \qquad}$ RESIDENTIAL-SCHOOL,

14. $\overline{\quad \text{t} \quad}$ MONEY,

15. $\overline{\qquad \text{t} \qquad}$ SIGN LANGUAGE,

16. $\overline{\quad \text{t} \quad}$ COLLEGE,

■ EXERCISE IV

Sign the following short paragraph. Using your voice and without signing, ask your partner the questions that follow the selection. Your partner should sign the answer back to you.

$\overline{\qquad \text{t} \qquad}$
WASHINGTON, RECENTLY MY SISTER VISIT. SHE SEE

$\overline{\qquad\qquad \text{n} \qquad\qquad}$
COLLEGE NAME H-O-W-A-R-D. SHE ENJOY WASHINGTON. COLD. FUTURE, SHE VISIT F-L-A. SHE THINK WILL ENJOY F-L-A. F-L-A HOT.

1. Where did my sister visit?

2. When?

3. Did she like it? Why or why not?

4. Which college did she see?

5. When will she visit Florida?

6. Does she think she will like it?

LESSON 7

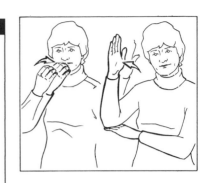

Imperatives and Using Numbers

1. When counting from 1 to 5 items, the palm faces inward to the signer.
2. When indicating age, the sign OLD followed by a number is used.
3. When a number accompanies the sign TIME as in TIME 5 (to mean 5 o'clock), the palm faces outward.

■ SET I
Practice Sentences

1. YOU-GIVE-ME 3 PENCIL.

2. TOMORROW I GO-AWAY TIME 10.

3. I FINISH PLAN 2 LESSON.

4. BUY 4 PLANT, PLEASE.

5. MY BROTHER AGE 30.

6. YOU-SEND-ME PICTURE 4.

        t
7. YESTERDAY LUNCH, I DRINK COKE 5.

8. CLASS FINISH TIME 3:15.

        t
9. HOMEWORK, WRITE 3 ADVERTISEMENT.

10. MY PARENTS DINNER TIME 5. I PREFER 6:30.

■ NOTES

Imperatives and Using Numbers

1. When counting from 1 to 5 items, the palm faces inward to the signer.
2. When indicating age, the sign OLD followed by a number is used.
3. When a number accompanies the sign TIME as in TIME 5 (to mean 5 o'clock), the palm faces outward.

■ SET II
Practice Sentences

1. BUY 7 TICKET.

2. I HAVE LEFT STAMP 2.

3. ORDER 3 HAMBURGER, 4 FRENCH-FRIES, PLEASE.

4. YESTERDAY I BUY C1:L̈L̈ 4.

5. I HAVE BROTHER AGE 7, SISTER AGE 5.

6. TO-TELEPHONE ME TIME 4:30 TOMORROW.

7. YESTERDAY MY BROTHER EAT HAMBURGER 3.

8. YOU-SEND-HER MOTHER 5 PLANT.

9. I AGE 59. JOHN, HE HE-ASK-ME MY AGE. I I-TELL-HIM 49. HE BELIEVE ME!

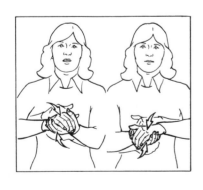

10. TOMORROW I STAY HOME UNTIL TIME 3 AFTERNOON.

■ *NOTES*

Personal Pronouns Incorporating Number and Plurals

Personal Pronouns Incorporating Number and Plurals

There are several ways to make plurals. Two alternatives are as follows:
1. Add a number before or after the noun.
2. Add a quantifier such as MANY, A-FEW, or SEVERAL before or after the noun.

■ SET I

Practice Sentences

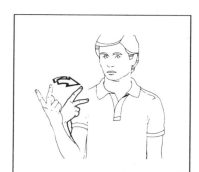

    t   t
1. PAUL (right), JOHN (left) TWO-OF-THEM AGE 10.

2. FIVE-OF-THEM FROM CALIFORNIA.

          t
3. CLASS FINISH, THREE-OF-YOU STAY.

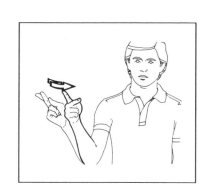

4. JOHN, I, TWO-OF-US TAKE-UP SIGN LANGUAGE.

          q
5. FOUR-OF-YOU AGE 14?

6. MY MOTHER HAVE COAT MANY.

7. YOU-GIVE-ME FEW PENCIL, PLEASE.

8. JOHN FIND SEVERAL B-U-S TICKET.

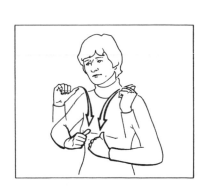

         t
9. FINGERSPELLING TEST, I MISTAKE MANY.

10. I COOK HAMBURGER FEW.

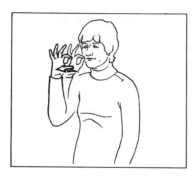

Personal Pronouns Incorporating Number and Plurals

There are several ways to make plurals. Two alternatives are as follows:

1. Add a number before or after the noun.
2. Add a quantifier such as MANY, A-FEW, or SEVERAL before or after the noun.

■ SET II

Practice Sentences

1. YESTERDAY MY SISTER, I, TWO-OF-US VISIT GRANDMOTHER.

2. FOUR-OF-US FROM O-H-I-O.

3. THREE-OF-US WANT WATER. THREE-OF-THEM WANT MILK.

4. TWO-OF-THEM HAVE EYES BROWN.

5. FIVE-OF-US UNDERSTAND.  HE UNDERSTAND.

   (annotation above "HE UNDERSTAND": n)

6. TODAY SEVERAL PEOPLE SICK.

7. YESTERDAY I WRITE SENTENCE MANY.

8. MY AUNT HAVE CAT SEVERAL.

9. I FINISH SEE MANY MOVIE.

10. YESTERDAY JOHN, HE HE-TEACH-ME SIGN FEW. I ENJOY.

■ EXERCISE I

Sign two sentences . . .

1. in which one sentence is a command and includes the sign *"GO-WITH"*.

2. in which one sentence includes the sign *"FIVE-OF-THEM"*.

3. with a "stuck-up" facial expression in which one sentence includes the sign *"12"*.

4. with a surprised facial expression in which one sentence includes the signs *"AGE 7"*.

5. in which one sentence is in the word order, *"OBJECT + SUBJECT + VERB"*, and includes the sign *"COKE"*.

6. in the past tense in which one sentence uses the sign *"FINISH"* to show that the action has been completed.

7. with an exasperated facial expression in which one sentence includes the signs *"TIME 6"*.

8. in which one sentence includes the directional verb *"YOU-GIVE-CL:C-ME"*.

9. in the future tense.

10. in which one sentence asks a yes/no question.

11. in which one sentence in English would start, *"DIDN'T . . . ?"*.

12. in which one sentence includes the sign *"DON'T-LIKE"*.

Exercises

■ EXERCISE II

Sign a sentence for each of the following words. Make the words plural by either adding a number or by adding the sign "MANY", "SEVERAL", or "A-FEW".

1. COATS
2. ADVERTISEMENTS
3. STAMPS
4. SPOONS
5. PLANTS
6. WRIST-WATCHES
7. PANTS
8. LETTERS
9. COOKIES
10. DOGS
11. CHAIRS
12. CARS
13. BOOKS

■ EXERCISE III

Pick two students in the class to sign Dialogue 2 on page 79 of *A Basic Course in American Sign Language.* To test comprehension, ask the class to answer the following questions:

1. Does Betty know Jack's brother?

2. Who are "good friends"?

3. What did Jack find out about Betty's sister?

4. How long has it been since Jack has seen Betty's sister?

5. What will Betty give Jack?

■ EXERCISE IV

Sign something that you do at the following times:

Example: TIME 8 FRIDAY NIGHT

I WANT DANCE TIME 8 FRIDAY NIGHT.

1. NOON
2. TIME 5 AFTERNOON
3. TIME 2 AFTERNOON
4. TIME 8 MORNING
5. TIME 6 NIGHT
6. TIME 12 FRIDAY NIGHT
7. TIME 7 MORNING
8. TIME 9 NIGHT
9. TIME 6 MONDAY MORNING
10. TIME 10 MORNING

LESSON 8

WH-Questions

WH-questions ask for specific information. These questions use signs such as WHO, WHAT, WHEN, WHERE, WHY, WHICH, HOW, WHAT-FOR ('why'), HOW-MANY/HOW-MUCH. They are made by:
1. Squeezing the eyebrows together.
2. Moving the head slightly forward.
3. Looking directly at the person being asked the question.

■ SET I
Practice Sentences

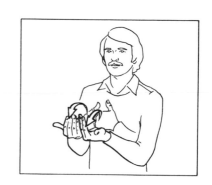

```
                whq
1. HOW-MUCH CANDY YOU HAVE?


             whq
2. WHERE BATHROOM WHERE?


          whq
3. DRAW PICTURE WHY?


          whq            q        q    whq
4. YOU WANT WHICH, ICE CREAM, CANDY, WHICH?


       whq         q
5. HOW YOU FEEL? SICK?


                  whq
6. YOU HAVE CHILDREN HOW-MANY?
```

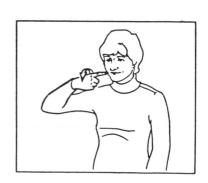

```
    whq
7. NAME YOU?


      whq       q
8. LONELY WHO? YOU?


             whq
9. HOW-MUCH FOOD LEFT?


                 whq
10. YOU BUY SEVERAL PANTS WHAT-FOR?
```

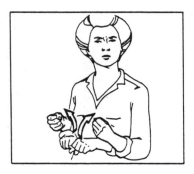

WH-Questions

WH-questions ask for specific information. These questions use signs such as WHO, WHAT, WHEN, WHERE, WHY, WHICH, HOW, WHAT-FOR ('why'), HOW-MANY/HOW-MUCH. They are made by:
1. Squeezing the eyebrows together.
2. Moving the head slightly forward.
3. Looking directly at the person being asked the question.

■ SET II
Practice Sentences

whq

1. WHO MADE COOKIE WHO?

whq

2. ALBERT FINISH BECOME DOCTOR WHEN?

whq

3. WHAT BREAK WHAT?

whq

4. WHO INFORM-YOU?

whq   q

5. WHEN CHILD RUN-AWAY? YESTERDAY?

whq

6. WORK WHERE YOU?

whq

7. YOU FIND WHAT?

whq

8. HOW-MANY HOUR YOU STUDY HOW-MANY?

whq

9. YESTERDAY WHAT-TO-DO YOU?

whq

10. TIME?

The SELF Pronoun

The SELF pronoun has two functions:
1. It can function as a reflexive pronoun.
2. It can function as another form of personal pronoun.

■ SET I

Practice Sentences

1. MYSELF COOK HAMBURGER YESTERDAY.

   $\overline{\hspace{4em}\text{whq}\hspace{4em}}$
2. HIMSELF BUY HORSE HOW-MANY?

3. OURSELVES CLEAN-UP.

4. YOURSELF GO-WITH MOTHER.

5. I WANT TALK-TO MAN MYSELF.

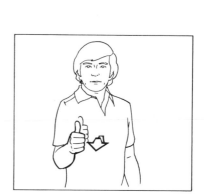

6. MYSELF MISTAKE.

7. YOURSELF YOU-SEND-HIM MAN ADVERTISEMENT.

   $\overline{\hspace{3em}\text{n}\hspace{3em}}$
8. NOT YOU YOU-ASK-HIM. I WANT I-ASK-HIM MYSELF.

   $\overline{\hspace{3em}\text{q}\hspace{3em}}$
9. HERSELF HAVE COAT 3?

10. MYSELF I-INFORM-YOU.

■ *NOTES*

The SELF Pronoun

The SELF pronoun has two functions:
1. It can function as a reflexive pronoun.
2. It can function as another form of personal pronoun.

■ SET II

Practice Sentences

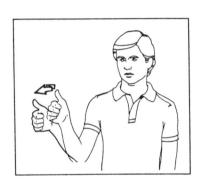

1. YOURSELF YOU-ASK-HER TEACHER.

2. MYSELF LUNCH TIME 12.

3. HIMSELF READ BOOK MANY.

4. MYSELF PLAN PARTY.

5. I I-SEND-YOU LETTER MYSELF.

                                     whq
6. YOURSELF NEED MONEY HOW-MUCH?

7. YOURSELF YOU-EXPLAIN-HER PAT.

8. MYSELF I-FORCE-YOU SIGN.

                                     q
9. YOUR DAUGHTER BUY PANTS HERSELF?

10. BROTHER, HIMSELF AGE 7.

■ *NOTES*

■ EXERCISE I

Have your partner respond as you ask a question . . .

1. which includes the sign *"WHO"* at the end of the sentence.

2. with an angry facial expression which includes the sign *"HOW"*.

3. looking drunk which starts, *"WHERE . . .?"*.

4. which ends with the sign *"HOW-MANY"* and includes the sign *"I-GIVE-YOU"*.

5. which starts, *"WHAT . . .?"*.

6. with a suspicious facial expression which starts and ends with the sign *"WHY"*.

7. which starts and ends with the sign *"WHERE"* and includes the sign *"TWO-OF-US"*.

8. which includes the *"WH-MARKER"* but does not use a *"WH"* word.

Sign two sentences . . . .

1. in which one sentence includes the sign *"5"*.

2. with a satisfied facial expression in which one sentence incudes the sign *"MANY"*.

3. with a firm facial expression in which one sentence includes the sign *"YOURSELF"*.

4. in the past tense in which the first sentence includes the sign *"FINISH"*.

5. in which one sentence commands someone to do something.

6. with a shocked facial expression in which one sentence includes the sign *"I-PAY-YOU"*.

7. in which one sentence is made negative without using the sign "*NOT*".

8. with a cautious facial expression in which one sentence refers to a person who is not present.

■ EXERCISE II

After studying the following sentences, sign them as quickly as possible using the facial expression indicated in the parentheses. Have your partner copy exactly what you have signed, including your facial expression.

1. $\overline{\text{I DON'T-WANT EAT HAMBURGER,}}^{\text{n}}$

   $\overline{\text{FRENCH FRIES TOMORROW!}}^{\text{n}}$ (Angry)

2. SORRY. I EXPLAIN WRONG. (Very apologetic)

3. I I-TELL-YOU FINISH GO-WITH MOTHER NOW! (Firm and Angry)

4. $\overline{\text{HER DRESS,}}^{\text{t}}$ UGLY! (Disgusted)

5. $\overline{\text{YOURSELF DECIDE?}}^{\text{q}}$ (Shocked and Questioning)

6. $\overline{\text{YESTERDAY YOU LEAVE TIME 8 WHY?}}^{\text{whq}}$ (Angry)

7. $\overline{\text{COFFEE,}}^{\text{t}}$ TASTE BAD. (Disappointed)

8. $\overline{\text{BOOK,}}^{\text{t}}$ $\overline{\text{YOU READ FINISH?}}^{\text{q}}$ (Shocked)

9. BEFORE FRIDAY I FEEL SICK. (Sick)

10. $\overline{\text{I NOT INTRODUCE YOU?}}^{\text{nq}}$ (Surprised)

Exercises

■ EXERCISE III

Ask your partner to sign the following vocabulary words to you:

SKILL	INFORM	OH-I-SEE	KNOW
LONELY	FORCE	WORD	PRACTICE
ADVERTISEMENT	CHALLENGE	WRONG	YELLOW
AFTER	MINUTE	YOUNG	MONEY
FACE	HOMEWORK	HUNGRY	PARENTS
PICTURE	GO-AWAY	LANGUAGE	TEACHER
INFLUENCE	DOCTOR	WINTER	COOL

Sign the following words to your partner and have your partner tell you the English equivalent:

STRONG	FOR	ALL-NIGHT	ANSWER
LIGHT (weight)	DIALOGUE	IMPROVE	MEAT
SAD	COLOR	LATER	LOOK-AT
INTERESTING	ABOUT	WALK	TUESDAY
FAMILY	THANK-YOU	USED-TO	PLAN
GOOD-FRIEND	WHITE-PERSON	WEAR	SEVERAL
CHILD	NEED	AGAIN	LEFT

■ EXERCISE IV

Sign three sentences using "DOG" as the topic.

1. _____

2. _____

3. _____

50

■ *NOTES*

LESSON 9

Noun-Verb Pairs

There are many nouns and verbs which are related to each other in meaning and form and differ only in movement. These are called noun-verb pairs. Some verbs have a single movement and the related noun has a smaller, repeated movement.

■ SET I
Practice Sentences

1. JACK, PUT-ON-HEARING-AID!

2. MY HEARING-AID BREAK.

3. $\overline{\text{COMB WHERE}}^{\text{whq}}$?

4. $\overline{\text{RAIN}}^{\text{t}}$, $\overline{\text{YOU LIKE}}^{\text{q}}$?

5. TODAY RAIN.

6. $\overline{\text{STORY C-I-N-D-E-R-E-L-L-A}}^{\text{t}}$, MY FAVORITE.

7. JACKIE SKILL TELL-STORY.

8. $\overline{\text{WINDOW}}^{\text{t}}$, $\overline{\text{YOU WASH FINISH}}^{\text{q}}$?

9. OPEN-THE-WINDOW.

10. BUY BOOK NAME A B-A-S-I-C C-O-U-R-S-E I-N AMERICAN SIGN LANGUAGE.

■ NOTES

Noun-Verb Pairs

There are many nouns and verbs which are related to each other in meaning and form and differ only in movement. These are called noun-verb pairs. Some verbs have a single movement and the related noun has a smaller, repeated movement.

■ SET II

Practice Sentences

1. OPEN-BOOK PAGE 6.

   _____whq_____
2. WORK WHERE YOU?

3. BEFORE MONDAY, I WORK.

   ___t___   _____q_____
4. RING, YOU BUY FINISH?

5. TO-TELEPHONE ME TOMORROW NIGHT TIME 6.

6. YESTERDAY MY SISTER BUY TELEPHONE NEW . . . . BLUE.

7. SIT DOWN!

8. YESTERDAY MY NIECE BIRTHDAY. I I-GIVE-HER RING.

9. JOHN PUT-ON-RING JUDY.

   _____t_____   _____q_____
10. REDSKINS, YOU FAVOR?

■ *NOTES*

Exercises

◼ EXERCISE I

Sign two sentences . . .

1. in which one sentence uses the sign *"RAIN"* as a noun.

2. in which one sentence uses the sign *"RAIN"* as a verb.

3. in the future tense with a tired facial expression.

4. with a mistrusting facial expression in which one sentence ends, *" . . . .WHY?"*.

5. with a terrified facial expression in which one sentence would start in English, *"ARE . . . . ?"*.

6. in which one sentence includes the sign *"BOOK"*.

7. in which one sentence includes the sign *"OPEN-BOOK"*.

8. in which one sentence ends with the sign *"HERSELF"*.

9. in which one sentence refers to two people who are not present.

10. in which one sentence uses the subject, *"MY GRANDMOTHER"*, as the topic.

11. in which one sentence starts, *"MYSELF . . . . "*.

12. in which one sentence includes the sign, *"FOUR-OF-US"*.

13. in which one sentence asks a yes/no question and starts, *"YOURSELF . . . . ?"*.

14. with a shocked facial expression in which one sentence includes the signs *"HAMBURGER 3"*.

15. in which one sentence includes the sign *"WARM"*.

■ LESSON 9

Exercises

■ EXERCISE II

Sign a sentence using each of the following subjects as topics:

1. CALIFORNIA
2. MEETING
3. LIBRARY
4. CANDY
5. FLOWER

6. STORE
7. TELETYPEWRITER
8. TEST
9. PURSE
10. COP

■ EXERCISE III

Name and describe your favorite person.

_____

_____

_____

■ EXERCISE IV

Sign the following sentences to your students. Have each student take turns adding information until a story is generated.

Recently I to-telephone my friend. Two-of-us talk. I surprised. She she-tell-me _____

(I recently called my friend. We talked. I was surprised. She told me _____)

Basic Sentence Structure:
Using Modals and Negative Modals

The modals that can accompany other verbs in a sentence are: CAN, SHOULD, MUST, WILL, FINISH, MAYBE. Some negative modals are: CAN'T, NOT-YET, REFUSE. There are three types of sentence structure with modals:
1. The modal is at the end of the sentence.
2. The modal precedes the verb.
3. The modal both precedes the verb and is repeated at the end of the sentence.

■ SET I
Practice Sentences

1. $\overline{\underline{}t}$ BOX, TOMORROW YOU YOU-SEND-HER $\overline{q}$ CAN YOU?

2. $\overline{q}$ CAN TWO-OF-US GO-AWAY B-E-A-C-H?

3. $\overline{n}$ I REFUSE GET-UP TIME 5 MORNING REFUSE!

4. GRANDFATHER VISIT C-L-E-V-E-L-A-N-D FINISH.

5. $\overline{y}$ TOMORROW I STUDY 1-HOUR WILL I!

6. LEAVE TIME 6:15 SHOULD YOU.

7. TOMORROW YOU YOU-GIVE-ME STAMP MUST!

8. TYPE HOMEWORK FINISH.

9. $\overline{n}$ YOUR FRIEND SHOW-UP NOT-YET.

10. JOHN AND I MAYBE MARRY.

Basic Sentence Structure: Using Modals and Negative Modals

The modals that can accompany other verbs in a sentence are: CAN, SHOULD, MUST, WILL, FINISH, MAYBE. Some negative modals are: CAN'T, NOT-YET, REFUSE. There are three types of sentence structure with modals:
1. The modal is at the end of the sentence.
2. The modal precedes the verb.
3. The modal both precedes the verb and is repeated at the end of the sentence.

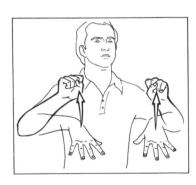

■ SET II

Practice Sentences

1. I CAN RIDE-BICYCLE.

2. $\overline{\text{LETTER}}$, YOU YOU-SEND-HER MUST.
   t above LETTER

3. $\overline{\text{PARTY}}$, I PLAN FINISH.
   t above PARTY

4. YOU MUST PRACTICE SIGN MUST!

5. $\overline{\text{UMBRELLA}}$, $\overline{\text{TOMORROW SHE SHE-GIVE-YOU WILL.}}$
   y   y

6. $\overline{\text{SHE SEE PERFORMANCE NOT-YET?}}$
   nq

7. $\overline{\text{MEETING SET-UP NOT-YET.}}$
   n

8. $\overline{\text{CAN'T TAKE-UP SIGN LANGUAGE CAN'T.}}$
   n

9. $\overline{\text{TEST DRIVE}}$, $\overline{\text{PASS WILL I.}}$
   t   y

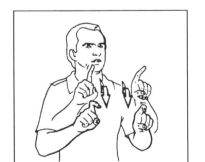

10. MEMORIZE SPEECH NAME "*G-E-T-T-Y-S-B-U-R-G A-D-D-R-E-S-S*" MUST YOU.

■ EXERCISE I

Sign two sentences . . .

1. in which one sentence includes the modal *"WILL"* at the end of the sentence.

2. with a satisfied facial expression in which one sentence includes the sign *"COOL"*.

3. in which one sentence includes the modal *"REFUSE"* both before the verb and at the end of the sentence.

4. in which one sentence uses the sign *"PARTY"* as the object in the *"OBJECT + SUBJECT + VERB"* word order.

5. in which one sentence asks a question and includes the modal *"CAN'T"*.

6. with a sad facial expression in which one sentence uses the signs *"MAN ACT-AGENT"* (actor) as the topic.

7. in which one sentence includes the classifier *"CL:CC"*.

8. in which one sentence includes the sign *"GIVE-TICKET"*.

9. with a *"drunk"* facial expression in which one sentence ends with the sign *"MYSELF"*.

10. in which one sentence commands someone to do something and which includes the sign *"YOU-GIVE-CL:C-HER"*.

11. with a questioning facial expression in which one sentence includes the sign *"HE-SHOW-YOU"*.

12. in which one sentence includes the signs *"3 BICYCLE"*.

13. in which one sentence ends with the sign *"WHICH"*.

■■■ **LESSON 10**

Exercises

■ EXERCISE II

Pick two students in the class to sign Dialogue 3 on page 109 of *A Basic Course in American Sign Language.* To test comprehension, ask the students to answer the following questions:

1. Did Tom see the movie?

2. Who is George Veditz?

3. What does Jack notice about Veditz' signing?

4. How much money did the NAD collect?

5. Why did they collect the money?

■ EXERCISE III

Sign a series of questions in which you use each of the modals (including the negative modals). Have your partner respond to your questions.

■ EXERCISE IV

Sign a short story about what you would do with $1,000,000.

■LESSON11■

Verbs Incorporating Location and Using Finish as a Conjunction

Some verbs change their movement to indicate a change from one location to another.

When used as a conjunction, FINISH means 'then.' It is often used to link sentences occurring in a time sequence.

■ SET I
Practice Sentences

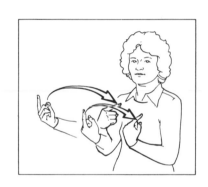

     <u> t </u>   <u> t </u>
1. S.F. (right), L.A. (left), I DRIVE-TO-S.F. (from home) FINISH,
                            <u> t </u>
   DRIVE-TO-L.A. (from S.F.). CAR, LEFT (in L.A.), FLY-TO-
   HERE HOME.

       <u> t </u>
2. STORE (right), I WALK-TO-STORE, BUY FOOD FINISH,
   WALK-TO-HERE HOME.

        <u> t </u>
3. SCHOOL (right), RECENTLY I BRING-TO-SCHOOL 5
        <u> t </u>
   BOOK. 2, STEAL; LEFT 3.

            <u> t   </u>   <u> t </u>
4. MY FRIEND HER HOUSE (right), SCHOOL (left), CLOSE.
   BEFORE, SHE YOUNG, WALK-TO-SCHOOL, WALK-TO-
   HOME (from school).

                               <u> t </u>
5. I LIVE N.J. (right), WORK N.Y. (left). MORNING, DRIVE-TO-
               <u> t </u>
   N.Y. (from N.J.) AFTERNOON, DRIVE-TO-N.J. (from N.Y.).

6. I GO-THERE LIBRARY (right), STUDY FINISH, COME-TO-
   HERE HOME, EAT.

7. I WORK 1-HOUR FINISH, GO-TO MOVIE.

8. I EXPLAIN MARY FINISH, SHE EXPLAIN YOU.

9. I TELL-STORY FINISH, YOU SLEEP. $\overline{\text{O.K.}}^{\text{q}}$?

10. I LECTURE FEW MINUTES FINISH, YOU (plural) TAKE-UP TEST.

■ *NOTES*

Verbs Incorporating Location and Using Finish as a Conjunction

Some verbs change their movement to indicate a change from one location to another.

When used as a conjunction, FINISH means 'then.' It is often used to link sentences occurring in a time sequence.

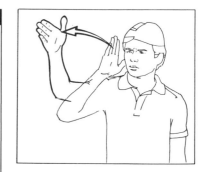

■ SET II
Practice Sentences

        <u>   t   </u>   <u>   t   </u>

1. CHICAGO (right), N.Y. (left), I WANT TO-BICYCLE-TO-N.Y. (from Chicago).

2. I READ BOOK FINISH, I GO-TO YOUR HOUSE.

3. I COOK DINNER, CLEAN-UP FINISH, EAT.

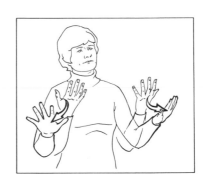

             <u>   t   </u>

4. RESTAURANT THERE (point right), YESTERDAY SISTER, BROTHER, I EAT THERE FINISH, GO-TO FOOTBALL GAME (left).

            <u>   t   </u>

5. TELEPHONE NUMBER, I I-GIVE-YOU FINISH, YOU TO-TELEPHONE.

   <u> t </u>

6. S.F. (right), FUTURE I MOVE-TO, WAIT 1-WEEK FINISH, TRY FIND JOB.

7. BEFORE SUMMER, I DRIVE-TO MY SISTER HOUSE (right), VISIT 1-WEEK FINISH, I FLY-TO F-L-A. (left) MY PARENTS LIVE THERE.

8. TOMORROW I DRIVE-TO RESIDENTIAL-SCHOOL (right). HAVE MEETING WITH SON TEACHER.

9. BEFORE SATURDAY MY FRIEND MARRY. I DRIVE-TO
   BOYFRIEND HOUSE (right) FINISH, TWO-OF-US
   DRIVE-TO CHURCH (left).

            t
   _____
10. MEETING (right), I URGE YOU (plural) GO-TO.

■ *NOTES*

Exercises

■ EXERCISE I

Sign two to three sentences . . .

1. in which one sentence includes the sign *"THERE"*.

2. with a disappointed facial expression in which one sentence includes the sign *"THAT"*.

3. in which one sentence includes the sign *"FINISH"* as a conjunction.

4. in which the first sentence starts, $\overline{\ \ \ \ t\ \ \ \ }$ *"PHILADELPHIA,. . . "* and includes a verb incorporating location.

5. in which one sentence includes the sign *"TWO-OF-US"*.

6. in which one sentence uses the subject as the topic.

7. with a delighted facial expression in which one sentence includes the sign *"FINISH"* to show that an action has been completed.

8. in which the first sentence starts, $\overline{\ \ \ t\ \ \ }$ *"CHURCH, . . ."* and includes a verb incorporating location.

9. with an excited facial expression in which one sentence includes the sign *"FINISH"* as a conjunction.

10. with a confused facial expression in which one sentence includes the sign *"WHERE"*. Pick another student to answer the question.

11. with a disgusted facial expression in which one sentence includes the modal *"CAN'T"*.

12. in which one sentence includes the sign *"3"*.

13. with a bored facial expression in which one sentence uses the sign *"FINISH"* as a conjunction and includes a verb incorporating location.

14. in which one sentence includes the sign *"HERE"*.

15. with an excited facial expression in which one sentence includes the sign *"DRIVE-TO"*.

■ EXERCISE II

Sign three to four sentences about a place to which you have either driven, flown, or walked.

_____

_____

_____

■ EXERCISE III

Complete the following sentences using an appropriate facial expression:

     <u> t </u>
1. CHURCH (right), I GO-TO FINISH, _____ .

2. I EAT FINISH, _____ .

   <u> t </u>
3. STORE (right), I DRIVE-TO FINISH, _____ .

       <u> t </u>   <u> t </u>
4. WASHINGTON (right), L.A. (left), _____ .

Exercises

_____

       <u>   t   </u>

5. BASEBALL GAME (right), I WALK-TO FINISH, _____ .

      <u> t </u>

6. LETTER, I WRITE FINISH, _____ .

      <u>   t   </u>

7. SIGN LANGUAGE, I PRACTICE FINISH, _____ .

      <u>   t   </u>

8. MY SISTER, HER HOUSE (right), _____ .

      <u>   t   </u>

9. RESTAURANT (point right), _____ .

      <u> t </u>   <u> t </u>

10. NEW YORK (right), PHILADELPHIA (left) _____ .

■ EXERCISE IV

Fingerspell the vocabulary from Lesson 10 and have your
partner sign the word that you have fingerspelled back to you.

■ *NOTES*

LESSON 12

Locational Relationships and Adding Movement to Pronominal Classifiers

Pronominal classifiers can be used to show locational relationships such as "on," "under," "behind," "in front of," "beside," "facing each other," "on top of," etc.
The action of persons or objects can be indicated by adding movement to pronominal classifiers.

■ SET I
Practice Sentences

Use your classifiers to show the following spacial arrangements or movement.

1. MY CAR IS NEXT TO YOUR CAR.

2. THE VAN IS BEHIND THE BLUE CAR.

3. A MAN IS STANDING BEHIND A WOMAN.

4. A CHILD IS STANDING ON A TABLE.

5. MY CUP IS NEXT TO THE PAPER.

6. A LEAF IS UNDER THE TREE.

7. I FOLLOWED THE BUS IN MY CAR.

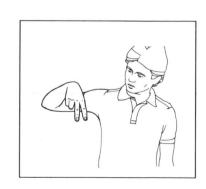

8. MY CAR WAS PARKED OVER THERE, AND A BUS CAME RIGHT UP BEHIND IT AND BUMPED IT.

9. DO YOU SEE THE CAR OVER THERE AND THE BOY STANDING NEXT TO IT? HE'S CUTE.

10. I WAS SITTING READING A BOOK. I GOT UP AND WALKED TO THE REFRIGERATOR.

Locational Relationships and Adding Movement to Pronominal Classifiers

Pronominal classifiers can be used to show locational relationships such as "on," "under," "behind," "in front of," "beside," "facing each other," "on top of," etc.
The action of persons or objects can be indicated by adding movement to pronominal classifiers.

■ SET II
Practice Sentences

Use your classifiers to show the following spacial arrangements or movement.

1. Did you park behind my car?

2. The boy standing next to the car, is that Jeff?

3. The glass is next to the book.

4. I want the blue glass behind the plate.

5. My bed and my sister's bed are at right angles to each other.

6. Open the door that is next to the table.

7. Ben is standing next to the window.

8. The glass was lying on its side on the table. I picked it up and righted it.

9. My friend is mad. He was standing under a tree. I walked up to him. He turned around and walked away.

10. Over there is a beautiful green and red kite flying above.

Exercises

■ EXERCISE I

Sign two to three sentences . . .

1. with an excited facial expression in which one sentence includes the classifier *"CL:3"*.

2. in which one sentence includes the sign *"DRIVE-TO"*.

3. in the present tense in which one sentence includes the sign *"TODAY"*.

4. in which one sentence includes the classifier *"CL:∧"* and the signs *"AUNT MARTHA"*.

5. in which one sentence uses the sign *"FINISH"* as a conjunction.

6. in which one sentence uses the subject *"SUNSET"* as the topic.

7. with a questioning facial expression in which one sentence includes the sign *"THAT-ONE"*.

8. in which one sentence includes the classifier *"CL:B"*.

9. in which one sentence uses the sign *"FINISH"* to show that the action has been completed.

10. in which one sentence refers to someone who is present and someone who is not present.

11. with a happy facial expression in which one sentence sets up *"CHICAGO"* on the right.

12. in which one sentence asks a question and includes the modal *"SHOULD"*.

13. in which one sentence includes the sign *"WHITE"* as an adjective following the noun.

14. in which one sentence includes the sign *"DON'T-KNOW"*.

15. in which one sentence includes the classifier *"CL:F"*.

■ LESSON 12

Exercises

16. in which one sentence uses the sign "HAVE" to indicate existence.

17. with a surprised facial expression in which one sentence uses the sign "HAVE" to show possession.

18. with a stern facial expression in which one sentence includes the signs "YOU MUST".

■ EXERCISE II

Sign two to three sentences in which you use one of the classifiers to show action.

_____

_____

_____

■ EXERCISE III

Sign the following paragraphs to your partner. When you are finished, ask your partner five questions based on the story. If possible, sign your questions. Your partner should answer in sign language.

TOMORROW I FLY-TO N.Y. (right). MY GIRLFRIEND LIVE THERE. I STAY ONE-WEEK, VISIT FINISH, R-E-N-T CAR DRIVE-TO WASHINGTON, D.C. (left) (from N.Y.). I TAKE-UP CLASS SIGN LANGUAGE ONE-WEEK AND MAYBE TAKE-UP CLASS

                    t
         _____
DRAWING. CLASS FINISH, FLY-TO-HERE HOME.

                 t
        _____
MY GIRLFRIEND HOUSE (right), YESTERDAY NIGHT I WALK-TO, EAT DINNER—HAMBURGER, FRENCH FRIES FINISH, TWO-OF-US DRIVE-TO MOVIE (left). SAD. I CRY . . . . . . FINISH, DRIVE-TO-HER-HOUSE FINISH, I WALK-TO-HERE HOME.

■ EXERCISE IV

Use your classifiers to show that something is _____
_____ something else. Be specific as to
what that something is.

                                    t
        Example: ON   ‾TABLE‾, BOOK C1:B (on).

1. BEHIND

2. NEXT TO

3. ON TOP OF

4. IN FRONT OF

5. AT RIGHT ANGLES TO

6. FACING

7. SLIGHTLY OVERLAPPING

8. UNDER

9. FAR AWAY FROM

10. FACING AWAY FROM

■ *NOTES*

LESSON 13

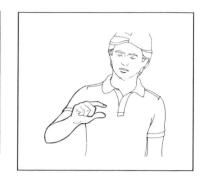

Mass Quantifiers

The quantifiers SOME, A-LITTLE, and PLENTY are added either before a mass noun or at the end of the sentence. Some classifiers also serve as quantifiers.

■ SET I

Practice Sentences

1. I MUST READ BOOK CL:G.

2. DESK HAVE PAPER CL:BB↑↓, CL:BB↑↓.

3. TODAY GET LETTER CL:Ḷ.

4. SOME PEOPLE ARRIVE EARLY.

5. I EAT PIE A-LITTLE.

$$\overline{}^{\,t}$$
6. PRESIDENT CAR, HAVE WINDOW CL:G!

7. I BUY DINNER. I HAVE MONEY PLENTY.

8. I MUST CORRECT PAPER CL:Ḷ.

9. MY FRIEND BRING SOME MAGAZINE YESTERDAY.

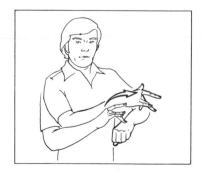

Mass Quantifiers

The quantifiers SOME, A-LITTLE, and PLENTY are added either before a mass noun or at the end of the sentence. Some classifiers also serve as quantifiers.

■ SET II

Practice Sentences

1. CL:BB←⟶(shelf) HAVE BOOK CL:BB ↑ ↓ .

2. SIGN LANGUAGE BOOK CL:Ḧ! WOW!

3. I MAKE COOKIE CL:ḦḦ, CL:G.

4. COME MY HOUSE, EAT. I HAVE FOOD PLENTY.

      _____t_____
5. MY LECTURE, I PRACTICE A-LITTLE.

6. MILK CL:Ḧ HAVE CREAM CL:G.

7. BOOKSTORE HAVE FINGERSPELL BOOK CL:Ḧ.
      _____q_____
      THAT-ONE IT I SHOULD BUY?

8. SOME MAN PREFER TALL WOMAN.

9. MY N-O-T-E-B-O-O-K CL:Ḧ!

      _____t_____
10. SIGN LANGUAGE, MY SON KNOW A-LITTLE.

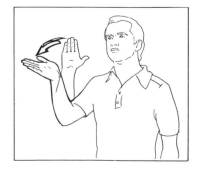

■ EXERCISE I

Sign two to three sentences . . . .

1. in which one sentence includes the signs *"17 DOLLAR"*.

2. with a frightened facial expression in which one sentence uses the sign *"CL:3"* on both hands.

3. in which one sentence includes the sign *"WINDOW+ +"*.

4. in which one sentence commands someone to do something.

5. in which one sentence includes the signs *"OLD 12"*.

6. in which one sentence uses the sign *"FINISH"* as a conjunction.

7. in which one sentence includes the sign *"6 DOLLAR"*.

8. with a disgusted facial expression in which one sentence includes the sign *"CHEESE"*.

9. with a disappointed facial expression in which one sentence asks a negative yes/no question.

10. in which one sentence includes the mass quantifier *"CL:G"* and the signs *"GLASS HAVE"*.

11. in which one sentence refers to someone who is not present.

12. in which one sentence asks a yes/no question and includes the sign *"TWO-OF-US"*.

13. in the past tense.

14. in which one sentence starts *"UNCLE JOE, HE . . . "*.

15. in which one sentence begins and ends with the sign *"HOW-MANY"*.

■ LESSON 13

Exercises

■ EXERCISE II

Sign a sentence for each of the following words listed below. Make these words plural in one of the following ways: adding a number (example: paper 3), using the sign "*CL:5*", or reduplicating the sign.

1. LISTS
2. CHILDREN
3. ROOMS
4. MAGAZINES
5. BOOKS
6. MACHINES
7. CHURCHES

8. CHAIRS
9. PLANTS
10. SUITCASES
11. HORSES
12. STAMPS
13. SHOES
14. BOTTLES

■ EXERCISE III

Pick two students in the class to sign Dialogue 4 on page 145 of *A Basic Course in American Sign Language.* To test comprehension, ask the class to answer the following questions:

1. What kind of group has been established in L.A.?

2. How many seats should be left for the performance?

3. How much do the tickets cost?

4. What is their agenda for that evening?

5. What day and time will they meet?

■ EXERCISE IV

Sign three or four sentences about your favorite hobby or activity.

_____

_____

_____

LESSON 14

Negatives

There are other ways to form negative sentences:
1. Use of NEVER. NEVER occurs either before the verb or at the end of the sentence.
2. Use of NONE to mean 'not' or 'not at all.' Verbs like HAVE, SEE, UNDERSTAND, FEEL, HEAR, EAT, and GET are frequently negated with NONE. NONE may occur either before or after the verb, but when it occurs after the verb, the two signs are often blended together in a single, smooth movement.

Negative Quantifiers

1. NONE may also be used before a noun to show a zero quantity of the noun.
2. NOTHING is also used after a verb to indicate zero quantity.

■ SET I
Practice Sentences

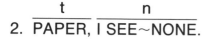

$$\overline{\text{JOHN WANT NONE HELP.}}^{\text{n}}$$
1. JOHN WANT NONE HELP.

$$\overline{\text{PAPER,}}^{\text{t}} \overline{\text{I SEE~NONE.}}^{\text{n}}$$
2. PAPER, I SEE~NONE.

$$\overline{\text{V-E-G,}}^{\text{t}} \overline{\text{I EAT NONE.}}^{\text{n}}$$
3. V-E-G, I EAT NONE.

4. MY SISTER RECENTLY MOVE.
$$\overline{\text{HER FURNITURE ARRIVE NOT-YET.}}^{\text{n}}$$
$$\overline{\text{SHE HAS FURNITURE NOTHING!}}^{\text{n}}$$

$$\overline{\text{I NEVER DEPEND MY PARENTS.}}^{\text{n}}$$
5. I NEVER DEPEND MY PARENTS.

_____t_____ _____n_____
6. COOKIE BLUE, I SEE NEVER.

_____n_____
7. THAT MONKEY LAZY. HE PLAY NOTHING.

_____n_____
8. MY FATHER HEAR NOISE BASEMENT. I HEAR~NONE.

___t___ _____n_____
9. TEST, I NEVER MEMORIZE D-A-T-E.

_____n_____
10. YESTERDAY MY DOG DIE. SINCE I FEEL~NONE.

_____n_____
11. THAT TEACHER PLAN LESSON NEVER.

_____n_____
12. FUTURE 20 MINUTE WE LEAVE. YOU PACK NOTHING!

_____n_____
13. BEFORE FRIDAY I HAVE NONE HOMEWORK.

___t___ _____n_____
14. RULE + +, MY SISTER NEVER OBEY.

_____n_____
15. MY PARENTS HAVE PATIENCE NOTHING.

■ *NOTES*

Negatives; Negative Quantifiers

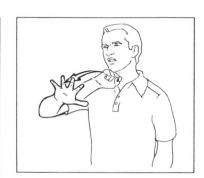

Negatives

There are other ways to form negative sentences:

1. Use of NEVER. NEVER occurs either before the verb or at the end of the sentence.
2. Use of NONE to mean 'not' or 'not at all.' Verbs like HAVE, SEE, UNDERSTAND, FEEL, HEAR, EAT, and GET are frequently negated with NONE. NONE may occur either before or after the verb, but when it occurs after the verb, the two signs are often blended together in a single, smooth movement.

Negative Quantifiers

1. NONE may also be used before a noun to show a zero quantity of the noun.
2. NOTHING is also used after a verb to indicate zero quantity.

■ SET II

Practice Sentences

$$\overline{\qquad\qquad \overset{\text{n}}{\qquad} \qquad\qquad}$$
1. I HAVE NONE BOYFRIEND.

$$\overline{\qquad\qquad\qquad \overset{\text{n}}{\qquad}\qquad\qquad}$$
2. MY AUNT DECIDE HERSELF. DISCUSS NOTHING.

3. I HAMMER, HIT-FINGER-WITH-HAMMER (mime).
$$\overline{\overset{\text{n}}{\quad}}$$
FEEL~NONE. I SURPRISED!

$$\overline{\qquad\qquad\qquad \overset{\text{n}}{\qquad}\qquad\qquad\qquad}$$
4. I HEAR~NONE JOHN GLENN WANT BECOME
$$\overline{\overset{\text{n}}{\quad\quad}}$$
PRESIDENT.

$$\overline{\overset{\text{t}}{\quad}}\quad\overline{\qquad\overset{\text{n}}{\qquad}\qquad}$$
5. CAR, MY FRIEND WASH NEVER.

$$\overline{\text{n}}$$
6. SUE NONE SATISFIED.

$$\overline{\text{n}}$$
7. I TRY SMOKE NEVER.

$$\overline{\text{n}}$$
8. SINCE I SEE~NONE TV

$$\overline{\text{n}}$$
9. RESTAURANT HAVE HAMBURGER NOTHING.

$$\overline{\text{n}}$$
10. TIME 3, SINCE I WAIT MAN ANNOUNCE RACE . . . NONE.

$$\overline{\text{q}}\quad\overline{\text{n}}$$
11. YOU UNDERSTAND LECTURE? I UNDERSTAND~NONE.

$$\overline{\text{n}}$$
12. ALL-DAY I EAT NONE. NOW HEADACHE.

$$\overline{\text{t}}\quad\overline{\text{n}}$$
13. TYPE, I PRACTICE NEVER.

$$\overline{\text{n}}$$
14. MY DOG CHASE CAT NEVER.

$$\overline{\text{n}}$$
15. I HAVE NONE MONEY.

Use of NOTHING

In some sentences, NOTHING has the meaning of a denial of a precedent accusation. The accusation usually has a topic marker.

■ SET I

Practice Sentences

<pre>
        t   n
1. SELL YOUR CAT, NOTHING!
</pre>

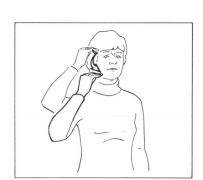

<pre>
                           t   n
2. BEFORE FRIDAY GO-WITH YOUR BOYFRIEND, NOTHING!
</pre>

<pre>
              t   n
3. CHALLENGE YOU BICYCLE RACE, NOTHING!
</pre>

<pre>
        t   n
4. EAT YOUR CANDY, NOTHING!
</pre>

<pre>
        t   n
5. SHAVE DOG HEAD, NOTHING!
</pre>

■ *NOTES*

Use of NOTHING

In some sentences, NOTHING has the meaning of a denial of a precedent accusation. The accusation usually has a topic marker.

■ **SET II**

Practice Sentences

$$\overline{\hspace{2.5cm}}^{\text{t}}\ \overline{\hspace{1.5cm}}^{\text{n}}$$
1. I STEAL MONEY, NOTHING!

$$\overline{\hspace{3cm}}^{\text{t}}\ \overline{\hspace{1.5cm}}^{\text{n}}$$
2. MY FATHER WEAR DRESS, NOTHING!

$$\overline{\hspace{2cm}}^{\text{t}}\ \overline{\hspace{1.5cm}}^{\text{n}}$$
3. FORCE JUDY LIE, NOTHING!

$$\overline{\hspace{3.5cm}}^{\text{t}}\ \overline{\hspace{1.5cm}}^{\text{n}}$$
4. I BREAK YOUR WRIST-WATCH, NOTHING!

$$\overline{\hspace{2cm}}^{\text{t}}\ \overline{\hspace{1.5cm}}^{\text{n}}$$
5. I I-BOTHER-YOU, NOTHING!

■ *NOTES*

Exercises

■ EXERCISE I

Sign two to three sentences . . . .

1. in which one sentence includes a classifier.

2. with a tired facial expression in which one sentence pluralizes the sign *"SUITCASE"*.

3. in which one sentence uses classifiers to show that something is behind something else.

4. in which one sentence includes the sign *"WATER"* and the mass quantifier *"CL:G"*.

5. with a mistrustful facial expression in which the first sentence starts, *"WHO . . . ?"*.

6. with a worried facial expression in which one sentence includes your vehicle passing a police car.

7. with a *"cool"* facial expression in which one sentence includes the sign *"NOT"*.

8. in which one sentence uses the sign *"HAVE"* to indicate existence.

9. with an amused facial expression in which one sentence includes a verb incorporating location.

10. with an upset facial expression in which one sentence includes an adjective before the noun.

11. in which one sentence uses the sign *"FINISH"* as a conjunction.

12. in which one sentence uses the sign *"FINISH"* to show that the action has been completed.

13. in which one sentence includes the sign *"NOTHING"*.

14. in which one sentence includes the sign *"SEE~NONE"*.

15. in which one sentence uses the sign *"NONE"* to mean *"ZERO QUANTITY OF"*.

16. in which one sentence uses the sign *"NEVER"*.

■ LESSON 14

Exercises

■ EXERCISE II

Complete the following sentences. The sign "NONE" should be used to show "ZERO QUANTITY OF" the noun.

Example: _____ MEET NONE _____ .

I MEET NONE CUTE WOMAN SINCE.

1. I WANT NONE _____ .

2. MY FATHER SEE NONE _____ .

3. YESTERDAY _____ EAT NONE _____ .

4. _____ COLLECT NONE _____ .

5. YOUR SISTER GET NONE _____ .

6. _____ BAKE NONE _____ .

7. _____ BUY NONE _____ .

8. _____ FIND NONE _____ .

9. _____ DRINK NONE _____ .

10. _____ HE-GIVE-ME NONE _____ .

■ EXERCISE III

Accuse your partner of five things and have him/her deny each accusation, and then switch roles.

■ NOTES

■ EXERCISE IV

Add a topic to these sentences:

1. $\overline{\quad\quad\overset{t}{\quad}\quad\quad}$, PAUL, HE SEE~NONE.

2. $\overline{\quad\quad\overset{t}{\quad}\quad\quad}$, MAN HEAR~NONE.

3. $\overline{\quad\quad\overset{t}{\quad}\quad\quad}$, TEACHER HAVE~NONE.

4. $\overline{\quad\quad\overset{t}{\quad}\quad\quad}$, MY GOOD-FRIEND FEEL~NONE.

5. $\overline{\quad\quad\overset{t}{\quad}\quad\quad}$, MY GRANDMOTHER GET~NONE.

6. $\overline{\quad\quad\overset{t}{\quad}\quad\quad}$, LAURIE, SHE UNDERSTAND~NONE.

7. $\overline{\quad\quad\overset{t}{\quad}\quad\quad}$, I HEAR~NONE.

8. $\overline{\quad\quad\overset{t}{\quad}\quad\quad}$, MY PARENTS GET~NONE.

9. $\overline{\quad\quad\overset{t}{\quad}\quad\quad}$, THIS MAN HAVE~NONE.

10. $\overline{\quad\quad\overset{t}{\quad}\quad\quad}$, MY BOYFRIEND UNDERSTAND~NONE.

86

■ *NOTES*

■LESSON 15

Directional Verbs

Some directional verbs such as CHOOSE, COPY, TAKE, SUMMON, TAKE-ADVANTAGE-OF, and BORROW have a movement opposite of other directional verbs such as GIVE, TELL, SHOW, ASK, INFORM.

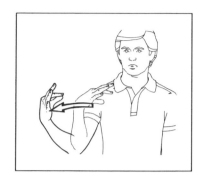

■ SET I
Practice Sentences

1. $\overline{\quad\text{t}\quad}$
   SENTENCE, YOU PUT-DOWN. I I-COPY-YOU.

2. TOMORROW DANCE S-A-D-I-E H-A-W-K-I-N-S.
   $\overline{\qquad\qquad\text{q}\qquad\qquad}$
   I-BORROW-YOU YOUR DRESS BLUE,
   $\overline{\quad\text{q}\quad}$
   SHOES BLACK CAN I?

3. $\overline{\quad\quad\text{t}\quad\quad}$
   COMMITTEE, IT-PICK-ME LECTURE.

4. $\overline{\quad\text{t}\quad}$
   TEST, BEFORE MONDAY I TAKE-UP. JOE HE HE-COPY-ME.

5. $\overline{\qquad\qquad\text{q}\qquad\qquad}$
   YOU THINK FRED WANT HE-TAKE-ME PARTY?

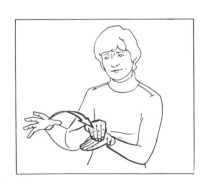

6. BEFORE MONTH I TRY JOIN BASEBALL TEAM. . . .
   $\overline{\quad\text{n}\quad}$
   NOT IT-PICK-ME.

■ NOTES

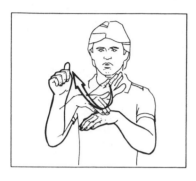

■ LESSON 15

Directional Verbs

Directional Verbs

Some directional verbs such as CHOOSE, COPY, TAKE, SUMMON, TAKE-ADVANTAGE-OF, and BORROW have a movement opposite of other directional verbs such as GIVE, TELL, SHOW, ASK, INFORM.

■ SET II

Practice Sentences

1. _____t_____
   WORK FINISH, YOU-SUMMON-ME. TWO-OF-US GO-AWAY B-E-A-C-H.

2. _____q_____
   YESTERDAY I SICK. CAN I I-COPY-YOU YOUR N-O-T-E-S? THANK YOU.

3. BEFORE MONTH YOU YOU-BORROW-ME MY HAMMER. NOW MONTH YOU YOU-BORROW-ME MY SCREWDRIVER.
   _____q_____
   NOW YOU WANT YOU-BORROW-ME MY WRENCH? YOU YOU-TAKE-ADVANTAGE-ME.

4. CHUCK, ED, TONY, I, FOUR-OF-US FEEL LECTURE BORING. THREE-OF-THEM THEY-PICK-ME TELL LECTURE-AGENT.

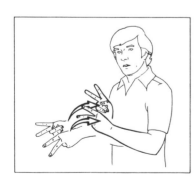

5. _____t_____
   DINNER READY, YOU-SUMMON-ME.

6. _____q_____
   YOU YOU-TAKE-ME DANCE?

___

■ *NOTES*

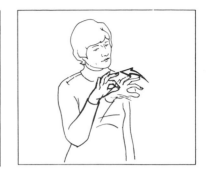

Directional Verbs Incorporating Two Objects

Directional verbs can change their movement to show the number of persons or objects.

◼ SET I
Practice Sentences

1. I WILL ARRIVE TIME 6 MORNING, YOU-TELL-TWO-THEM.

2. I FINISH I-ASK-TWO-THEM.

       t   t
3. MY CAR, YESTERDAY TWO-OF-THEM WASH. 5-DOLLAR, I I-GIVE-TWO-THEM.

                         q
4. THAT MAN HE-CHOOSE-ME, HE-CHOOSE-YOU?
      whq
WHAT-FOR?

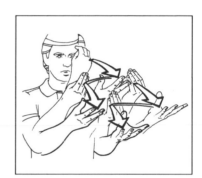

      t
5. USE SIGN, I I-FORCE-TWO-THEM, WILL I.

◼ NOTES

■■■ **LESSON 15**

Directional Verbs Incorporating Two Objects

Directional Verbs Incorporating Two Objects

Directional verbs can change their movement to show the number of persons or objects.

■ **SET II**

Practice Sentences

1. JANE, SHE SHE-PICK-TWO-THEM BECOME LEAD-AGENT.

2. I WANT I-SHOW-YOU-TWO.

         t
3. MY PICTURE, I I-SEND-TWO-THEM FINISH.

      t   t
4. COKE, I I-GIVE-YOU-TWO-CL:C. BEER, I-GIVE-YOU-TWO-CL:C. (Use four people in the classroom)

        t
5. MONEY, I I-BORROW-TWO-THEM. I I-TAKE-ADVANTAGE-TWO-THEM.

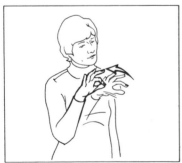

■ *NOTES*

Directional Verbs Incorporating EACH or ALL

Directional Verbs Incorporating EACH or ALL

Directional verbs also change to indicate 'to each of you/ them,' or 'to all of you/them.'

■ SET I
Practice Sentences

1. TEACHER SHE SHE-ASK-EACH-OF-YOU FINISH.

          t   q
2. RING ENGAGEMENT, I I-SHOW-ALL-OF-YOU FINISH?

                               q
3. GAME CANCEL . . . RAIN. I I-TELL-ALL-OF-YOU FINISH?

4. TOMORROW I DECIDE. I I-INFORM-ALL-OF-YOU.

       t
5. 3-DOLLAR, AFTERNOON I I-PAY-EACH-OF-YOU.

       t
6. MY DECISION, TOMORROW I I-INFORM-EACH-OF-YOU.

7. I SUGGEST WE LEAVE TOMORROW. THEY THEY-ALL-TELL-ME THEY PREFER LEAVE TONIGHT.

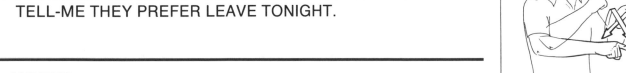

■ *NOTES*

Directional Verbs Incorporating EACH or ALL

Directional verbs also change to indicate 'to each of you/ them,' or 'to all of you/them.'

■ SET II
Practice Sentences

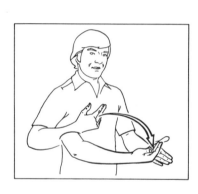

t

1. <u>SCHOOL FINISH</u>, I I-INFORM-EACH-OF-YOU G-R-A-D-E.

2. I FINISH I-TELL-ALL-OF-YOU, ARRIVE TIME 10 MUST.

t

3. <u>MY SHIRT FROM CALIFORNIA</u>, I WANT I-SHOW-ALL-OF-YOU.

4. YESTERDAY I I-TELL-ALL-OF-YOU, COME RIGHT TIME MUST.

5. BEFORE SATURDAY I I-LOAN-EACH-OF-YOU $3.00.

6. YOU YOU-BORROW-EACH-OF-US—STOP-IT!

7. NONE YOU (plural) STUDY. I I-GIVE-ALL-OF-YOU MORE HOMEWORK.

■ *NOTES*

Exercises

■ EXERCISE I

Sign two to three sentences . . .

1. in which one sentence includes the sign *"I-GIVE-EACH-OF-YOU"*.

2. in which one sentence includes the sign *"NOTHING"*.

3. in which you respond to the accusation, *"YOU BREAK MY CAMERA!"*.

4. in which one sentence includes the mass quantifier *"CL:BB↑↓"*.

5. in which one sentence includes the sign *"GET~NONE"*.

6. in which one sentence includes the signs $\overline{\text{"RICKY}}$ (right), $\overline{\text{BOB}}$ (left), I I-ASK-TWO-THEM".

7. in which one sentence includes the classifier *"CL:3"* and the fingerspelled word *"V-A-N"*.

8. in which one sentence includes the sign *"APPOINTMENT"* as the object in the *"OBJECT + SUBJECT + VERB"* word order.

9. in which you look like you are smothering laughter.

10. in which one sentence starts, *"MY FRIEND JANE, SHE . . ."*.

11. in the past tense in which one sentence includes the sign *"I-TAKE-ADVANTAGE-HER"*.

12. in which one sentence includes the sign *"SHE-SHOW-ALL-OF-YOU"*.

13. in which one sentence includes the sign *"HAIR"*.

14. in which one sentence commands someone to do something and includes the modal *"MUST"*.

■ *NOTES*

15. in which one sentence includes the signs, *"LISA, SHE-CHOOSE-ME"*.

■ EXERCISE II

Sign the following sentences to your students. Have each student take turns adding information until a story is generated.

Yesterday I do-work homework. Hear noise kitchen. Get-up, walk-to-kitchen kitchen (right). (shocked facial expression) . . . . ! ! ! !

(Yesterday I was doing my homework. I heard a noise in the kitchen. I got up and walked to the kitchen. I saw . . . . . ! ! ! !)

■ EXERCISE III

Think of something that someone listed below would ....

      Example: TEACHER—GIVE-TO-ALL-OF-THEM

           t
        ‾‾‾‾‾
       TEST, TEACHER GIVE-TO-ALL-OF-THEM.

1. CHILD—SHOW-EACH-OF-YOU.

2. MAN HIMSELF LOST—ASK-THEM-TWO.

3. MOTHER—SEND-EACH-OF-THEM.

4. LEAD-AGENT—INFORM-ALL-OF-YOU.

5. PRESIDENT—TELL-ALL-OF-YOU.

6. MAN—LOOK-AT-EACH-OF-THEM.

7. UNCLE—LEND-YOU-TWO.

8. THAT STUDENT—COPY-YOU-TWO.

9. BEAUTIFUL GIRL—TAKE-ADVANTAGE-EACH-OF-THEM.

10. TEACHER—HELP-ALL-OF-THEM.

LESSON 16

Time Measurements and Tense Indicators Incorporating Number

The time signs MINUTE, HOUR, DAY, WEEK, and MONTH (but not YEAR) incorporate the numbers 1–9.
The tense indicators NEXT-WEEK, LAST-WEEK, NEXT-MONTH, NEXT-YEAR, and LAST-YEAR can also incorporate some numbers. But they vary in which numbers they can incorporate.

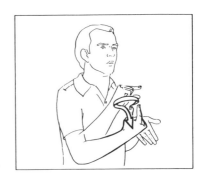

■ SET I

Practice Sentences

1. SINCE 6-MONTH I WORK TEACHER. ENJOY.

2. LAST-YEAR MY SISTER MOVE-TO F-L-A. NEXT-YEAR SUMMER I DRIVE-THERE, VISIT. STAY 2-WEEK FINISH, DRIVE-TO HOME.

3. $\overline{\text{LAST-WEEK YOU YOU-TELL-ME YOUR NAME?}}^{\text{q}}$

4. 3-YEAR-AGO MY BOYFRIEND, I WALK, SEE CAR-ACCIDENT.

5. SINCE 8-WEEK I SICK. $\overline{\text{STUDY}}^{\text{t}}$, DIFFICULT.

6. 2-WEEK-AGO I BUY BACKPACK.

7. IN-6-MONTH I MARRY.

8. 4-YEAR-AGO I GRADUATE COLLEGE.

9. SINCE 3-YEAR NONE MONEY INCREASE. I DISAPPOINT.

10. YOU PLAY CONTINUE 5-MINUTE FINISH, YOU SLEEP.

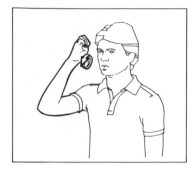

Time Measurements and Tense Indicators Incorporating Number

The time signs MINUTE, HOUR, DAY, WEEK, and MONTH (but not YEAR) incorporate the numbers 1–9.
The tense indicators NEXT-WEEK, LAST-WEEK, NEXT-MONTH, NEXT-YEAR, and LAST-YEAR can also incorporate some numbers. But they vary in which numbers they can incorporate.

■ **SET II**

Practice Sentences

1. I WAIT 2-HOUR FOR B-U-S. FINALLY ARRIVE. I ANGRY.
    <u>   t   </u>
    B-U-S DRIVE-AGENT, I I-BAWL-OUT-HIM.
    <u>   n   </u>
    HE DON'T-CARE.

2. <u>   t   </u>
    EARN ENOUGH MONEY BUY THAT COAT, MUST WORK 3-DAY.

3. MY BABY BORN IN-4-MONTH.

4. I MEET YOUR BROTHER 3-WEEK-AGO. NICE, FRIENDLY.

5. IN-6-MONTH I JOIN DEAF BASEBALL TEAM.

6. 2-WEEK-AGO I LOAN YOU $5.00.

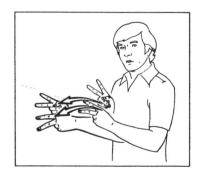

7. <u>   t   </u>
    TOMORROW SPEECH CLASS, I MUST LECTURE 3-MINUTE. I NERVOUS.

8. TODAY I INTERPRET 3-HOUR.

9. I WORK CONTINUE. IN-5-MINUTE YOU-SUMMON-ME.

10. 2-YEAR-AGO I GO-BY-BOAT EUROPE.

Time Reduplication and Repetition

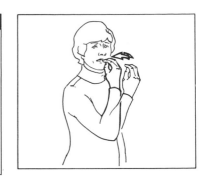

Time Reduplication and Repetition

The signs HOUR, WEEK, MONTH, and NEXT-YEAR can be reduplicated to mean 'hourly,' 'weekly,' 'monthly,' and 'yearly.' Some forms of time that occur regularly are not repeated but use a single movement.

■ SET I
Practice Sentences

1. EVERY-THURSDAY MY SISTER, BROTHER, I EAT TOGETHER. BEFORE THURSDAY EAT MY HOUSE. NEXT-WEEK THURSDAY EAT SISTER HOUSE. IN-2-WEEK THURSDAY EAT BROTHER HOUSE.

2. YEARLY YOU SHOULD GO DOCTOR.

3. WEEKLY I SPEND $50.00 FOOD.

4. EVERY-MONDAY NIGHT I EAT HAMBURGER.

5. DAILY LUNCH COST $3.

6. YEARLY MOUSE ENTER MY HOUSE.

7. EVERY-3-YEAR I DRIVE-TO CHICAGO, VISIT MY GOOD-FRIEND.

8. I TAKE-UP CLASS SCIENCE, MEET TIME 9 UNTIL 11 EVERY-SATURDAY.

9. EVERY-3-MONTH I GET MONEY INCREASE NAME "COST-O-F-LIVE".

■ NOTES

Time Reduplication and Repetition

The signs HOUR, WEEK, MONTH, and NEXT-YEAR can be reduplicated to mean 'hourly,' 'weekly,' 'monthly,' and 'yearly.' Some forms of time that occur regularly are not repeated but use a single movement.

■ SET II

Practice Sentences

$$\overline{q}$$
1. YOU EAT FISH EVERY-FRIDAY?

2. EVERY-2-YEAR I VISIT EUROPE.

3. I WANT WORK EVERY-SATURDAY.

4. EVERY-3-HOUR I MUST MILK (MIME MILKING) COW.

5. WEEKLY I MUST WRITE 15 SENTENCE.

6. DAILY WE LEARN NEW VOCABULARY.

7. EVERY-2-MONTH GALLAUDET COLLEGE OFFER CLASS

$$\overline{n}$$
SIGN LANGUAGE. I WISH JOIN. CAN'T. WORK.

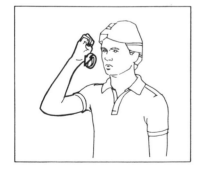

8. DAILY TIME 6 MORNING, 6 NIGHT, TAKE-PILL GREEN. EVERY-3-HOUR TAKE-PILL ORANGE. AWFUL.

9. MONTHLY I HAVE B-I-L-L CL:Ḷ̈.

■ EXERCISE I

Sign two to three sentences . . .

1. in which one sentence includes the sign *"IN-3-YEAR"*.

2. with an exasperated facial expression in which one sentence includes the sign *"MONTHLY"*.

3. in which one sentence includes the sign *"I-HELP-YOU-TWO"*.

4. in which one sentence includes the modal *"WON'T"* at the end of the sentence.

5. in which one sentence uses the subject *"WINTER"* as the topic.

6. in which one sentence uses the sign *"BASEMENT"* as the object in the *"OBJECT + SUBJECT + VERB"* word order.

7. in which one sentence includes the signs *"6 YEAR BEFORE"*.

8. in which one sentence includes the sign *"I-LOOK-AT-ALL-OF-YOU"*.

9. in which you respond to the accusation *"YOU LAZY, YOU!"*

10. in which one sentence includes the sign *"I-GIVE-CL:C-YOU"*.

11. in which one sentence sets up *"STORE"* on the right and *"SCHOOL"* on the left and includes a verb incorporating motion.

12. in which one sentence asks a yes/no question and includes the sign *"THERE"*.

13. in which one sentence sets up *"PHILADELPHIA"* on the right and uses the sign *"FINISH"* as a conjunction.

■■■■ **LESSON 16**

Exercises

14. with a confused facial expression in which one sentence includes the sign *"THAT"*.

15. in which one sentence includes the sign *"WHEN"*.

■ EXERCISE II

Sign several sentences about something you do regularly. Be sure to include in your facial expressions and body movements how you feel about it.

_____

_____

_____

_____

_____

■ EXERCISE III

After studying the following sentences, sign them as quickly as possible using the facial expression indicated in the parentheses. Have your partner copy exactly what you have signed, including your facial expression.

1. PUT-GAS-IN NOW! (Angry)

       _____t_____
2. MY BOOK, YESTERDAY STEAL. (Upset)

3. YESTERDAY NIGHT DINNER DELICIOUS. (Happy)

4. LOOK-AT-ME! (Demanding, Angry)

              ____whq____
5. JOHN CRY. WHAT'S-UP? (Upset)

      _____n_____   _____n_____
6. NOT YOU-FORCE-ME DRIVE. I DON'T-LIKE! (Nervous)

Exercises

---

7. PLEASE YOU YOU-HELP-ME. (Entreating)

$\overline{\quad\text{n}\quad}$

I UNDERSTAND. (Frustrated)

$\overline{\qquad\qquad\text{n}\qquad\qquad}$ $\overline{\text{q}\quad}$

8. I DON'T-WANT WORK AFTER SCHOOL. YOU? (Frustrated)

$\overline{\qquad\text{whq}\qquad}$

9. COOK WHAT, YOU? (Questioning, Excited) SMELLS
   DELICIOUS! (*"Mouth Watering"*)

10. I RECENTLY BUY BICYCLE. BEAUTIFUL. RED. (Excited)

■ EXERCISE IV

Pick three students to sign Dialogue 5 on page 175 of *A Basic
Course in American Sign Language*. To test comprehension,
ask the students to answer the following questions:

1. How many deaf people work with Ron?

2. Ron says that his co-workers don't know sign language.
   How does he hope to change this?

3. Has he been successful?

4. How many deaf people work at Jane's company?

5. Where are Ron and Bill and Jane?

■ *NOTES*

■ *NOTES*

LESSON 17

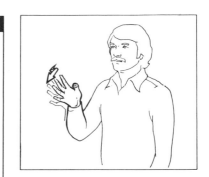

Comparative Sentences

When comparing two persons, places, things or ideas, the following procedure is used.
1. First establish one person, place, thing or idea on one side of the body and the other on the other side.
2. Then indicate which one you will comment upon.
3. A person, place, thing or idea can be established in a pronoun location to show a relationship with that pronoun.

■ SET I
Practice Sentences

1. $\overline{\text{WASH-DISH,}}^{\text{t}} \overline{\text{WASH-IN-MACHINE.}}^{\text{t}}$ (wash-dish) I PREFER.
   $\overline{\text{REASON,}}^{\text{t}} \overline{\text{DON'T-KNOW.}}^{\text{n}}$

2. $\overline{\text{NTID,}}^{\text{t}} \overline{\text{GALLAUDET,}}^{\text{t}}$ (Gallaudet) FARTHER.

3. $\overline{\text{HEAD-COLD,}}^{\text{t}} \overline{\text{HEADACHE,}}^{\text{t}}$ (headache) WORSE.

4. $\overline{\text{EAT HOME,}}^{\text{t}} \overline{\text{EAT RESTAURANT,}}^{\text{t}}$ (eat home) CHEAPER.

5. $\overline{\text{SNOW,}}^{\text{t}} \overline{\text{RAIN,}}^{\text{t}}$ (snow) MOST PEOPLE PREFER.

6. $\overline{\text{NEW CAR,}}^{\text{t}} \overline{\text{OLD CAR,}}^{\text{t}}$ (new car) QUIETER.

7. $\overline{\text{PANTS BLUE,}}^{\text{t}} \overline{\text{PANTS BROWN,}}^{\text{t}}$ (pants blue) SMALLER.

8. $\overline{\text{MY SISTER,}}^{\text{t}} \overline{\text{MY BROTHER,}}^{\text{t}}$ (my brother) SHYER.

Comparative Sentences

When comparing two persons, places, things or ideas, the following procedure is used.

1. First establish one person, place, thing or idea on one side of the body and the other on the other side.
2. Then indicate which one you will comment upon.
3. A person, place, thing or idea can be established in a pronoun location to show a relationship with that pronoun.

■ SET II

Practice Sentences

      <u>   t   </u> <u>   t   </u>
1. MY CHILD, YOUR CHILD, (my child) SMARTER.

      <u>   t   </u> <u>   t   </u>
2. EXERCISE DAILY, EXERCISE EVERY-2-DAY, (every-2-day) BETTER.

      <u> t </u> <u> t </u>
3. DOG, CAT, (dog) FRIENDLIER.

      <u>   t   </u> <u> t </u>
4. MY BROTHER, MY SISTER, (my sister) NICER.

      <u>   t   </u> <u> t </u>
5. INTERPRET, TEACH, (teach) RANDY PREFER.

      <u>   t   </u> <u>   t   </u>
6. RED CAR, ORANGE CAR, (orange car) I PREFER.

      <u>   t   </u> <u>   t   </u>
7. EAST U.S., WEST U.S., (West U.S.) DRYER.

      <u>   t   </u> <u>   t   </u>
8. MY SUITCASE, YOUR SUITCASE, (my suitcase) LIGHTER.

Conjunctions

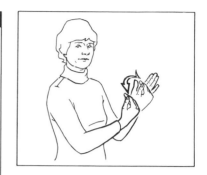

Conjunctions

The signs WRONG, HAPPEN, HIT, FRUSTRATE, and FIND can be used as conjunctions. Some of their meanings as conjunctions are:

WRONG 'without warning, suddenly'
FRUSTRATE 'to be prevented from'
HIT 'unexpectedly, turned out that'
FIND 'find out that'
HAPPEN 'happened that'

▰ SET I

Practice Sentences

1. $\overline{\quad\text{t}\quad}$
    NEWSPAPER, READ, HIT REMEMBER APPOINTMENT.

2. LAST-WEEK I BUY 6 FLOWER BEAUTIFUL, FRUSTRATE ALL DIE.

3. $\overline{\qquad\qquad\qquad\text{n}\qquad\qquad\qquad}$
    SINCE 6-MONTH NOT TO-TELEPHONE FRIEND. YESTERDAY, TO-TELEPHONE, FIND FRIEND MOVE N-E-B-R-A-S-K-A.

4. YEAR 1932, HAPPEN PEOPLE DEAF 300 MOVE-TO O-H-I-O.

5. I D-A-T-E JOE 5-MONTH, FIND HE FINISH MARRY.

6. PAUL, MARY MARRY 6-MONTH, HAPPEN DIVORCE.

7. YESTERDAY NIGHT I STUDY LESSON 6 AND 7. TODAY,
    $\overline{\qquad\text{n}\qquad}$
    FIND TEST LESSON 8 AND 9 NOT 6 AND 7.

8. 2-WEEK-AGO I GO BASKETBALL TOURNAMENT,
    $\overline{\qquad\text{n}\qquad}$
    FRUSTRATE CANCEL. NOT HE-INFORM-ME.

9. $\overline{\qquad\text{t}\qquad}$
    I DRIVE CL:3, WRONG CAR CL:3 (came up behind me and smashed into the back of my car).

■ **LESSON 17**

Conjunctions

Conjunctions

The signs WRONG, HAPPEN, HIT, FRUSTRATE, and FIND can be used as conjunctions. Some of their meanings as conjunctions are:

WRONG 'without warning, suddenly'
FRUSTRATE 'to be prevented from'
HIT 'unexpectedly, turned out that'
FIND 'find out that'
HAPPEN 'happened that'

■ SET II

Practice Sentences

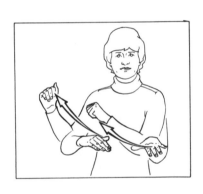

$$\overline{t}$$

1. B-A-N-K, NOW MORNING I GO-TO, FRUSTRATE CLOSE. FORGET, TODAY VACATION V-E-T-E-R-A-N DAY.

2. I SIT OUTSIDE, HIT, RAIN.

3. MY GIRLFRIEND, I, DISCUSS WHERE TO-BICYCLE. SHE SAY G-A-T-E-S M-I-L-L-S. I SAY C-H-A-G-R-I-N ROAD. DISCUSS FINISH, DECIDE G-A-T-E-S M-I-L-L-S. FINE. ARRIVE, FIND HER IDEA, G-A-T-E-S M-I-L-L-S, MY IDEA C-H-A-G-R-I-N ROAD SAME PLACE.

4. LAST-YEAR, HAPPEN MY BROTHER DIE.

5. BEFORE FALL I PLAN TAKE-UP SCIENCE CLASS, FRUSTRATE CANCEL.

6. I D-A-T-E WITH FRED, WRONG MIKE APPEAR!

7. BEFORE JUNE FINALLY FIND JOB. WORK 4-MONTH, HAPPEN C-O CLOSE.

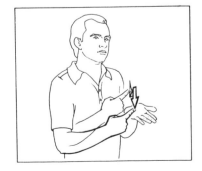

8. I PLAN INTERPRET MEETING, HIT SICK, $\overline{\text{CAN'T GO.}}^{\;n\;}$

9. MY FRIEND, I, DECIDE EAT LUNCH FAMOUS RESTAURANT. ARRIVE, FRUSTRATE CLOSE.

■ EXERCISE I

Sign two to three sentences. . . .

1. with an excited facial expression in which one sentence uses the sign *"HAPPEN"* as a conjunction.

2. in which you refer to two people who are not present.

3. in which one sentence compares a bicycle to a car.

4. in which one sentence uses the sign *"FRUSTRATE"* as a conjunction.

5. with a depressed facial expression in which one sentence includes the sign *"MONTHLY"*.

6. in which one sentence includes the classifier *"CL:B"*.

7. in which one sentence includes the signs *"HAVE MAGAZINE"*.

8. in which one sentence includes classifiers to show that something is on something else.

9. with a belligerent facial expression in which one sentence includes the modal *"REFUSE"*.

10. with a questioning facial expression in which one sentence includes the sign *"PUT-IN-GAS"*.

11. in which one sentence includes the sign *"3"*.

12. in which one sentence includes the sign *"TEND"* preceded
    by a topicalized clause: $\overline{}^{\;t}$　　　　, ... tend.

■ LESSON 17

Exercises

■ EXERCISE II

Translate the following paragraph into ASL:

Last year I earned a lot of money and decided to fly to Chicago. I went with my good frend, Debbie. We flew to Chicago Saturday morning. Saturday afternoon, we visited my girlfriend, Louse. She has lived in Chicago since 1980. Saturday night, Debbie and I ate at a restaurant near Lake Michigan. The food was delicious but expensive. It cost $63.00 for the two of us. Wow! After dinner, we went to a play. It was funny and enjoyable. Sunday afternoon, we went shopping, then rode the bus to the airport. At 3:00, we flew home. We enjoyed ourselves in Chicago and hope to visit Chicago again in the future.

■ EXERCISE III

1. Radio, TV
2. East, West
3. Chicago, Philadelphia
4. Europe, America
5. Bird, Horse
6. U.S. Government, S-t-a-t-e Government
7. President Reagan, President Carter
8. Nurse, Doctor
9. Interpret-agent (Interpreter), Teacher
10. Cat, Mouse
11. TV With Caption, TV With None Caption
12. Movie, TV
13. Word, Picture
14. Sick, Healthy
15. Baseball, Basketball

■ EXERCISE IV

Complete the following sentences using the conjunctions, "WRONG", "FRUSTRATE", "HIT", "FIND", "HAPPEN" or "FINISH":

1. I walk _____ .

2. I I-loan-him money _____ .

   _____t_____
3. California, I fly-to _____ .

4. Jackie plan take-up sign language _____ .

5. 3-hour I exercise _____ .

6. I bathe _____ .

   _____t_____
7. B-u-s, my uncle ride _____ .

8. 2-week-ago I buy car new. I drive C1:3 _____ .

9. My mother live Washington. I plan visit her in-2-week _____ .

10. Today have appointment doctor. I go. Fine. Arrive _____ .

11. My niece buy expensive furniture _____ .

12. Two-of-us discuss 3-hour _____ .

LESSON 18

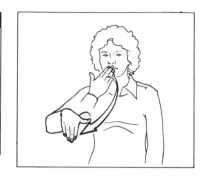

Verb Inflection: -REPEATEDLY

Many action verbs can be repeated to show a repeated or regular action. Frequently, facial adverbs are used with verbs inflected for -REPEATEDLY.

■ SET I

Practice Sentences

1. $\overline{\text{DRIVE TEST}}^{\text{t}}$, I FAIL-REPEATEDLY. (carelessly) FINALLY, BEFORE MONTH PASS.

2. MR. SMITH, HIMSELF TEACHER BAD.
   $\overline{\text{HE EXPLAIN NOTHING.}}^{\text{n}}$ I I-ASK-HIM-REPEATEDLY. (with attention)

3. COMPLAIN-REPEATEDLY. $\overline{\text{YOU SATISFIED NEVER.}}^{\text{n}}$

4. $\overline{\text{PAUL}}^{\text{t}}$ (right), $\overline{\text{HARRY}}^{\text{t}}$ (left), (to Paul) I EXPLAIN, HE

   UNDERSTAND. (To Harry) $\overline{\text{EXPLAIN-REPEATEDLY,}}$
   $\overline{\text{STILL UNDERSTAND NONE.}}^{\text{n}}$ (with attention)

5. MY DAUGHTER LOSE-REPEATEDLY HER WATCH. (carelessly)

6. $\overline{\text{WOMAN THERE}}^{\text{t}}$, THAT MAN HE-LOOK-AT-HER-REPEATEDLY. (with attention)

7. I MUST TAKE-PILL FOR STOMACH (point to stomach), TAKE-PILL FOR HEAD, TAKE-PILL FOR BACK (point to back). ALL-DAY, I TAKE-PILL-REPEATEDLY. (with effort)

LESSON 18

Verb Inflection: -REPEATEDLY

FINALLY, succeed

8. BEFORE, I YOUNG, MY GIRLFRIEND, ME, TWO-OF-US,

$\overline{\text{t}}$

LIBRARY GO-THERE-REPEATEDLY. (with ease)

$\overline{\hspace{2cm}\text{t}\hspace{2cm}}$

9. MY UNCLE LUCKY. MONEY, HE FIND-REPEATEDLY.

$\overline{\hspace{2cm}\text{t/n}\hspace{2cm}}$

10. REASON LEARN NOTHING SINCE, YOU GONE-
REPEATEDLY. (carelessly)

$\overline{\hspace{1cm}\text{t}\hspace{1cm}}$

11. MEETING, PEOPLE APPLAUD-REPEATEDLY. (with
attention)

12. MY FATHER SICK D-I-A-B-E-T-E-S. HE MUST GET-SHOT-
REPEATEDLY.

13. I I-TELL-HER MY FRIEND, I TO-TTY-HER THURSDAY.
THURSDAY I TO-TTY-HER-REPEATEDLY, FRUSTRATE

$\overline{\hspace{1cm}\text{n}\hspace{1cm}}$

SHE NOT HOME. (with effort)

■ *NOTES*

Verb Inflection: -REPEATEDLY

Many action verbs can be repeated to show a repeated or
regular action. Frequently, facial adverbs are used with verbs
inflected for -REPEATEDLY.

■ SET II

Practice Sentences

```
        t
     ‾‾‾‾‾‾
```
1. MONEY, I I-LOAN-YOU-REPEATEDLY. TOTAL $60.
```
                    whq
     ‾‾‾‾‾‾‾‾‾‾‾‾‾‾‾‾‾‾‾‾‾‾‾‾‾‾‾‾‾‾‾‾‾‾
```
   WHEN YOU YOU-PAY-ME B-A-C-K WHEN?

2. SINCE 3-WEEK I I-HELP-YOU-REPEATEDLY HOMEWORK.
```
                 n
       ‾‾‾‾‾‾‾‾‾‾‾‾‾‾‾‾‾‾
```
   (with effort) TODAY DON'T-WANT. SORRY.

3. MY GRANDMOTHER, ME ARGUE-REPEATEDLY. (with
   effort)

```
        t
     ‾‾‾‾‾‾
```
4. SENTENCE, I ANALYZE-REPEATEDLY. (with attention)
```
              n
     ‾‾‾‾‾‾‾‾‾‾‾‾‾‾‾‾‾‾
```
   STILL UNDERSTAND NONE.

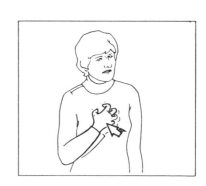

5. LAST-WEEK I VACATION. NOW WEEK PEOPLE TO-
   TELEPHONE-REPEATEDLY.

```
        t
     ‾‾‾‾‾‾
```
6. DANNY, I I-TELL-HIM-REPEATEDLY
```
               n
     ‾‾‾‾‾‾‾‾‾‾‾‾‾‾‾‾‾‾
```
   NOT TO-TELEPHONE AFTER TIME 10. (with effort)
   YESTERDAY NIGHT, HE TO-TELEPHONE TIME 11:15.
   I FED-UP.

```
        t
     ‾‾‾‾‾‾
```
7. MY CAR, MUST PUT-GAS-IN-REPEATEDLY. (with effort)

■■■■ ■ **LESSON 18**

Verb Inflection: -REPEATEDLY

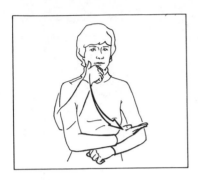

$$\overline{\hspace{3em}}^{t}\overline{\hspace{2em}}^{n}\overline{\hspace{2em}}$$

8. I ENJOY SPORTS. REASON, DON'T-KNOW. I LOSE-REPEATEDLY. (carelessly)

$$\overline{\hspace{4em}}^{n}\overline{\hspace{3em}}^{t}\overline{\hspace{1em}}$$

9. NOT TAKE-PILL-REPEATEDLY. (carelessly) BOTTLE, READ. (with attention)

10. I ANNOUNCE-REPEATEDLY.

$$\overline{\hspace{3em}}^{n}\overline{\hspace{3em}}$$

YOU PAY-ATTENTION NOTHING.

11. HER DAUGHTER COMPLAIN-REPEATEDLY.

12. SINCE 2-WEEK YOU YOU-BOTHER-ME-REPEATEDLY. STOP-IT!

$$\overline{\hspace{3em}}^{t}\overline{\hspace{2em}}$$

13. MY UNCLE HOUSE, I GO-THERE-REPEATEDLY. (with ease)

■ *NOTES*

Verb Inflection: -CONTINUALLY

Many verbs inflect by adding a circular movement to show a continuing action. Facial adverbs used with -REPEATEDLY can also be used with the -CONTINUALLY inflection.

■ SET I

Practice Sentences

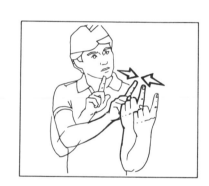

1. <u>   t   </u> <u> n/t </u>
   WORK-CONTINUALLY, NONE PLAY —BORING. (with attention)

2. YESTERDAY MY BIRTHDAY. MY FAMILY GO RESTAURANT. I EAT-CONTINUALLY. (with ease)

3. <u>   t   </u> <u>   n   </u>
   BEFORE, ME KID, CHURCH, I UNDERSTAND. SEEM
   <u>   n   </u>
   STAND-CONTINUALLY FOR NOTHING.

4. EVERY-SATURDAY MORNING, MY SISTER LOOK-AT-CONTINUALLY TV (with ease)

5. <u>   t   </u>
   GRADUATION, I INTERPRET-CONTINUALLY. (with
   <u>   t   </u>
   attention) FINISH, FEET (point to feet) HURT.

6. <u> t </u>
   PICTURE, I ANALYZE-CONTINUALLY. (with attention)

7. EVERY-MORNING THAT GIRL COMB-HAIR-CONTINUALLY 1-HOUR! (with attention)

8. MY FATHER PROMISE COME VISIT MY DAUGHTER. SHE
   <u>   n   </u>
   WAIT-CONTINUALLY. (with ease) FATHER NOT SHOW-UP.
   SHE CRY-CONTINUALLY. I I-PITY-HER.

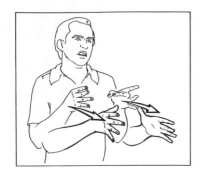

9. I ENJOY VISIT MY SISTER. I STAY-CONTINUALLY 2-HOUR. (with ease)

10. PAULA GOOD WORK-AGENT. SHE WORK-CONTINUALLY ALL-DAY. (with attention)

11. I HATE D-A-T-E. I MEET MAN. I I-GIVE-HIM TELEPHONE NUMBER. I WAIT-CONTINUALLY HIM TO-TELEPHONE.

          t
12. ‾‾‾‾‾‾‾‾‾‾‾‾‾‾ DOCTOR ROOM, I GO-TO SIT-CONTINUALLY. FINALLY, DOCTOR READY.

13. SINCE 2-WEEK HEADACHE-CONTINUALLY.

14. THAT TEACHER AWFUL. HE TALK-CONTINUALLY 3-HOUR. (carelessly)

          t
15. ‾‾‾‾‾‾‾‾‾‾‾‾‾‾ HOMEWORK, YESTERDAY NIGHT I STRUGGLE-CONTINUALLY. (with effort)

■ *NOTES*

Verb Inflection: -CONTINUALLY

Many verbs inflect by adding a circular movement to show a continuing action. Facial adverbs used with -REPEATEDLY can also be used with the -CONTINUALLY inflection.

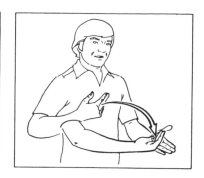

◼ SET II

Practice Sentences

1. $\overline{\overset{\text{n}}{\text{I EXERCISE NOTHING.}}}$ I SIT-CONTINUALLY ALL-DAY. (with ease)

2. I D-I-E-T. $\overline{\overset{\text{t}}{\text{BREAKFAST,}}}$ $\overline{\overset{\text{t}}{\text{LUNCH,}}}$ $\overline{\overset{\text{n}}{\text{I EAT~NONE.}}}$ FINE. BUT $\overline{\overset{\text{t}}{\text{NIGHT,}}}$ I EAT-CONTINUALLY. (carelessly)

3. $\overline{\overset{\text{t}}{\text{THAT MAN, EYES GREEN, BLOND,}}}$ HE HE-LOOK-AT-YOU-

   $\overline{\overset{\text{n}}{\text{CONTINUALLY.}}}$ (with attention) $\overline{\overset{}{\text{I NEVER MET HIM.}}}$

   $\overline{\overset{\text{q}}{\text{YOU KNOW HIS NAME?}}}$

4. I HAMMER-CONTINUALLY. (with attention)

   $\overline{\overset{\text{n}}{\text{NONE SUCCESS.}}}$

5. THAT WOMAN SMOKE-CONTINUALLY. (carelessly) (mime smoking)

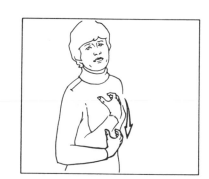

6. INTERPRET USE R-O-C-H-E-S-T-E-R M-E-T-H-O-D MEAN FINGERSPELL-CONTINUALLY. (with attention)

   $\overline{\overset{\text{n}}{\text{MANY DEAF PEOPLE DON'T-LIKE.}}}$ THEY SAY

   $\overline{\overset{\text{t}}{\text{FINGERSPELLING WATCH-CONTINUALLY,}}}$ BORING, EYES TIRED. (with attention)

7. YESTERDAY JOHN, HE HE-TELL-ME J-O-K-E. I LAUGH-CONTINUALLY.

8. SINCE 3-HOUR I WORK-CONTINUALLY. (with attention)

9. I HUNGRY. SCHOOL FINISH, I HURRY, ARRIVE HOME, EAT-CONTINUALLY WILL I.

10. $\overline{\text{BED}}^{\,t}$, YESTERDAY MORNING I STAY-CONTINUALLY. (with ease) $\overline{\text{TIME 11}}^{\,t}$, GET-UP.

11. $\overline{\text{RIDE B-U-S}}^{\,t}$ (right), $\overline{\text{DRIVE}}^{\,t}$ (left), I PREFER DRIVE— (point left). $\overline{\text{RIDE B-U-S}}^{\,t}$, (right) GET-UP EARLY, WALK-THERE, WAIT-CONTINUALLY. (with effort)

12. I VISIT MY AUNT. I STAY-CONTINUALLY. (with ease)

13. $\overline{\text{B-U-S}}^{\,t}$, I WAIT-CONTINUALLY. (with effort) FINALLY, ARRIVE.

14. I WORK-CONTINUALLY 1-HOUR, REST 15 MINUTE, WORK-CONTINUALLY 1-HOUR, REST 15 MINUTE. (with attention)

15. 2-HOUR I INTERPRET-CONTINUALLY. (with attention)

■ *NOTES*

Exercises

■ EXERCISE I

Sign two to three sentences . . .

1. in which one sentence includes the sign *"DOUBT"*
   preceded by a topicalized clause: $\overline{t}$, . . . doubt.

2. in which one sentence compares a volunteer with a paid worker.

3. in which one sentence includes the sign *"YEARLY"*.

4. in which one sentence includes the sign *"GO" -REPEATEDLY* with a facial expression showing *"WITH EASE"*.

5. in which one sentence refers to two people who are not present.

6. in the past tense in which one sentence includes the sign *"TELL" -REPEATEDLY*.

7. in which one sentence includes the sign *"NEVER"*
   preceded by a topicalized clause: $\overline{t}$, . . . never.

8. in which one sentence uses the sign *"CL:5̈"* to make a noun plural.

9. in which one sentence includes the adjective *"BIG"* following the noun.

10. in which one sentence includes the mass quantifier *"CL:BB ↑ ↓ "*.

11. in which one sentence includes the directional verb *"SHE-BAWL-OUT-HER"*.

12. in which one sentence includes the classifier *"CL:∧"* showing motion.

13. with a conspiring facial expression in which one sentence includes the verb *"TELL-STORY"*.

■ NOTES

14. in the future tense in which one sentence includes the directional verb *"I-SUMMON-YOU"*.

15. in which one sentence includes the sign *"STUDY"* - CONTINUALLY with a facial expression showing *"WITH ATTENTION"*.

■ EXERCISE II

Ask your partner the following questions for number or fingerspelling practice:

       whq
1. YOUR NAME?

          whq
2. WHERE YOU LIVE WHERE?

         whq
3. HOW-MANY YEAR LIVE THERE?

    whq
4. AGE YOU?

        whq
5. YOU BIRTHDAY WHEN?

       q
6. YOU HAVE CHILDREN?

     whq
A. HOW-MANY?

   t   t   whq
B. SON, DAUGHTER, WHICH?

     whq
C. THEIR NAME?

   whq
D. AGE?

           whq
7. WHO YOUR FAVORITE MAN ACT-AGENT WHO?

Exercises

───

_____whq_____
8. WHO YOUR FAVORITE WOMAN ACT-AGENT?

_____whq_____
9. WHICH C-O-U-N-T-Y YOU LIVE?

____t____ _____whq_____
10. BROTHER, YOU HAVE HOW-MANY?

___t___ ____whq____
11. SISTER, HOW-MANY?

_____whq_____
12. WHO GOOD-FRIEND YOU WHO?

___whq___
13. TIME?

_____whq_____
14. WHERE YOU BORN WHERE?

Think of 3 to 5 more questions to ask your partner to give him/her number of fingerspelling practice.

Fingerspell the following numbers and have your partner sign each number back to you:

1. 67
2. 39,000
3. 2,000,000
4. 12,650

5. 13
6. 90,000
7. 7,000,000
8. 50,203

Fingerspell the following words and have your partner sign each word back to you:

1. TALK
2. NEAR
3. SUNDAY
4. REST
5. WET
6. PROMISE
7. ENOUGH
8. RIGHT
9. BROTHER
10. APPOINTMENT

11. DOCTOR
12. SCARE
13. STRICT
14. FAULT
15. COMPETE
16. ACCEPT
17. LECTURE
18. MEMORIZE
19. COLLECT
20. RECOGNIZE

■ *NOTES*

■■■■■ **LESSON 19**

Adjective Modulation: VERY-

■ EXERCISE III

Tell your partner something that you do or that someone you know does. . . . .

1. repeatedly with ease and pleasure.

2. repeatedly to which close attention must be paid.

3. continually with effort or difficulty.

4. continually without attention or carelessly.

5. continually with ease and pleasure.

6. repeatedly with effort or difficulty.

7. continually to which close attention must be paid.

8. repeatedly without attention or carelessly.

LESSON 19

Adjective Modulation: VERY-

Adjectives can change their movement to add an adverbial meaning. The movement added to adjectives to mean 'VERY' has the following form:
1. The beginning of the sign has a hold which appears "tense."
2. Then there is a quick release.

■ SET I

Practice Sentences

1. I FEEL VERY-SICK. I THINK F-L-U.

2. MY FRIEND BUY HOUSE COST $13,000—VERY-CHEAP.

3. PEOPLE MANY WANT MOVE-TO A-R-I-Z-O-N-A. IT VERY-
$$\overline{\text{DRY.}}^{\,n}\;\text{ME. I PREFER EAST U.S.}$$

4. SINCE 4-MONTH I D-I-E-T—EAT 1,200 C-A-L-O-R-I-E-S DAILY. I VERY-HUNGRY.

5. MY TEACHER VERY-STRICT. SHE SHE-BAWL-OUT-ME-REPEATEDLY.

6. PEOPLE LIVE A-P-P-A-L-A-C-H-I-A VERY-POOR.

$$\overline{\hspace{4cm}}^{\,q}$$
7. YOUR SISTER AGE 16 MARRY NEXT-WEEK? SHE VERY-YOUNG!

8. MY AUNT, UNCLE RECENTLY MOVE-TO F-L-A. 3-WEEK-AGO I DRIVE-THERE, VISIT. VERY-HOT!
$$\overline{\hspace{4cm}}^{\,n}$$
MYSELF NEVER MOVE-THERE, NEVER.

9. MY NEIGHBOR RECENTLY MOVE-AWAY. NOW, HAVE NEW NEIGHBOR. HE VERY-LOUD! AWFUL.

10. LARRY, HIS SISTER HAVE DOG S-I-B-E-R-I-A-N H-U-S-K-Y. DOG VERY-WHITE.

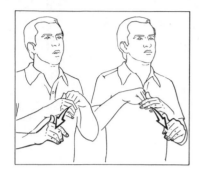

Adjective Modulation: VERY-

Adjectives can change their movement to add an adverbial meaning. The movement added to adjectives to mean 'VERY' has the following form:

1. The beginning of the sign has a hold which appears "tense."
2. Then there is a quick release.

■ SET II
Practice Sentences

                 q
1. YOU DECIDE GO DOCTOR? VERY-GOOD!

    t   t
2. B-U-S, 3-YEAR-AGO I RIDE-TO CHICAGO. AWFUL. B-U-S,
                        n
VERY-DIRTY, NOT COMFORTABLE.

          t   t
3. MY BOYFRIEND, VERY-CUTE. HAIR, VERY-BLACK,
    t
EYES, VERY-GREEN.

4. LISA, SHE SHE-TELL-ME J-O-K-E—VERY-FUNNY!

5. I VERY-ANGRY.

6. SOMETIMES I SIGN VERY-FAST. SORRY.

                              n
7. MY SISTER REFUSE SHE-LEND-ME HER BICYCLE. SHE
VERY-SELFISH.

8. THAT CANDY VERY-SOUR.

9. I FINISH BUY DRESS 4, PANTS 3, SHIRT 5. NOW I VERY-BROKE.

        t
10. FOOTBALL, MY BOYFRIEND LOOK-AT-REPEATEDLY.
VERY-BORING!

Adjective Modulation: -REPEATEDLY

Adjective Modulation: -REPEATEDLY

Some adjectives can be repeated to show the meaning of 'repeatedly.' This movement is added to adjectives which describe a temporary condition—in other words, a condition which can start, stop, and then start again.

■ SET I
Practice Sentences

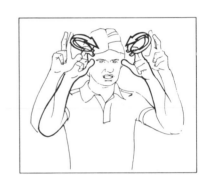

1. MY E-X BOYFRIEND ANGRY-REPEATEDLY. $\overline{\text{I DON'T-LIKE.}}^{\text{n}}$

2. MY NIECE MISCHIEVOUS-REPEATEDLY.

3. I WORRY-REPEATEDLY. I BECOME SICK U-L-C-E-R WILL.

4. I TRY FORCE-YOU (plural) SIGN, $\overline{\text{NONE TALK.}}^{\text{n}}$ STILL YOU TALK-REPEATEDLY. I FRUSTRATE-REPEATEDLY.

5. MY SISTER AND BROTHER LATE-REPEATEDLY.
$\overline{\text{CAN'T DEPEND THEM.}}^{\text{n}}$

6. $\overline{\text{YOU PAY-ATTENTION YOUR WORK,}}^{\text{t}}$ $\overline{\text{NEVER.}}^{\text{n}}$ YOU CARELESS-REPEATEDLY, WRONG-REPEATEDLY.

7. DAILY ROOM DIFFERENT-REPEATEDLY. TODAY 105, YESTERDAY 106, TOMORROW 107. FED-UP!

8. BEFORE I LIVE F-L-A. I HOT-REPEATEDLY. $\overline{\text{CAN'T BEAR.}}^{\text{n}}$ DECIDE MOVE-TO O-H-I-O. BETTER.

■■■■ **LESSON 19**

Adjective Modulation: -REPEATEDLY

Adjective Modulation: -REPEATEDLY

Some adjectives can be repeated to show the meaning of 'repeatedly.' This movement is added to adjectives which describe a temporary condition—in other words, a condition which can start, stop, and then start again.

■ **SET II**

Practice Sentences

1. MY DAUGHTER BECOME AGE 18, SHE ARRIVE HOME LATE-REPEATEDLY. I WORRY-REPEATEDLY.

2. BEFORE MONDAY, I TO-TELEPHONE MY FATHER. HE SICK, HEAD-COLD. HE SICK-REPEATEDLY.

3. DOOR (reduplicate) LEFT, BLUE-REPEATEDLY.

       <u>   t   </u>
4. WINTER, I COLD-REPEATEDLY.

       <u>   t </u>
5. WORK, SINCE 5-MONTH MY UNCLE LATE-REPEATEDLY.
<u>   t   </u>
YESTERDAY, FIRED.

    <u>   t </u>   <u>   q   </u>
6. TEST, YOU MISTAKE-REPEATEDLY?

            <u>   t   </u>
7. TEST FINGER SPELLING, MY TEACHER SHE SHE-GIVE-ME. I LOOK-AT (test), WRONG-REPEATEDLY.

8. MY CHILD AFRAID-REPEATEDLY.

Adjective Modulation: -CONTINUALLY

Adjective Modulation: -CONTINUALLY

Adjectives which describe a temporary condition can also be inflected to show the meaning of 'continually.' This inflection is made by adding a circular movement.

■ SET I
Practice Sentences

1. MY GIRLFRIEND MOVE-TO K-O-R-E-A LAST-YEAR. SINCE SHE SICK-CONTINUALLY.

2. THAT TEACHER MAD-CONTINUALLY. I THINK
   <u>   n   </u>
   SHE DON'T-LIKE CHILDREN.

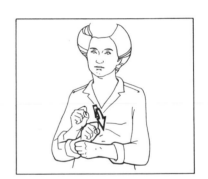

3. SINCE 2-WEEK MY ARM (point to arm) HURT-CONTINUALLY. TOMORROW, I GO DOCTOR. I HOPE HE HE-GIVE-ME PILL.

4. YESTERDAY MY NIECE, NEPHEW COME VISIT. THEY
   <u>   t   </u>
   MISCHIEVOUS-CONTINUALLY. MY SISTER ARRIVE, I RELIEVE.

5. LAST-WEEK MY BOYFRIEND MAD-CONTINUALLY.
   <u>   t   n   </u>
   REASON, I DON'T-KNOW. I THINK TROUBLE WORK.

6. MY VACATION TERRIBLE. I SICK-CONTINUALLY.

7. I SICK M-I-G-R-A-I-N-E. ALL-DAY HEADACHE-CONTINUALLY.

■ *NOTES*

▨ LESSON 19

Adjective Modulation: -CONTINUALLY

Adjective Modulation: -CONTINUALLY

Adjectives which describe a temporary condition can also be inflected to show the meaning of 'continually.' This inflection is made by adding a circular movement.

▪ SET II

Practice Sentences

        t
   ‾‾‾‾
1. M-A-Y, SINCE I SICK-CONTINUALLY.

2. YOU DRIVE-TO N.Y., YOU BE-CAREFUL-CONTINUALLY.

        t
   ‾‾‾‾‾‾‾‾
3. PEOPLE DEAF, SOME THINK LIP-READ FRUSTRATE-
CONTINUALLY.

4. SINCE I SICK-CONTINUALLY, FIND HAVE M-O-N-O-N-U-C-L-
E-O-S-I-S. 3-WEEK STAY HOME MUST.

             t
   ‾‾‾‾‾‾‾‾‾‾
5. SCIENCE CLASS, I WANT GIVE-UP. I FRUSTRATE-
CONTINUALLY.

6. BEFORE I LIVE NEW YORK CITY. I AFRAID-CONTINUALLY.
I MOVE. NOW LIVE N.J. BETTER.

            t
   ‾‾‾‾‾‾‾‾
7. PROBLEM 7, I STRUGGLE-CONTINUALLY.

▪ *NOTES*

Exercises

■ EXERCISE I

Sign two to three sentences. . . .

1. in which one sentence includes the sign "HABIT".

2. with a scared facial expression in which one sentence includes the sign "DANGER".

3. in which one sentence includes the sign "VERY-MAD".

4. in which one sentence inflects the verb to show continual action.

5. with a joyous facial expression in which one sentence includes the sign "CELEBRATE". One sentence should be in the "OBJECT + SUBJECT + VERB" word order.

6. in which one sentence inflects the verb to show repeated action.

7. in which one sentence includes the sign "DON'T-WANT" in

   the word order: $\overline{t}$, ... don't-want.

8. with a hopeful facial expression in which one sentence includes the sign "I-COPY-YOU".

9. in which one sentence uses the sign "FIND" as a conjunction.

10. in which one sentence includes the sign "I-TELL-EACH-OF-YOU".

11. in which one sentence includes the sign "NONE".

12. in which one sentence includes the mass quantifier "CL:L̈" and sign "SNOW".

13. in which one sentence includes the signs "TIME 8".

14. in which one sentence includes the sign "NOTHING".

15. in which one sentence would start, "ARE YOU. . . ?" in English.

■■■■ **LESSON 19**

Exercises

■ EXERCISE II

Sign a sentence using the following words with an appropriate facial expression:

1. very-strict
2. very-sophisticated
3. very-sweet
4. very-funny
5. very-frustrated
6. very-happy
7. very-relieved
8. very-loud
9. very-mischievous
10. very-lazy
11. very-red
12. very-cold
13. very-proud
14. very-tired
15. very-ugly

■ EXERCISE III

Translate the following story into ASL and sign it to your partner. When you are finished, ask your partner five questions based on the story.

You owe me money. Last fall you wanted to buy a new watch, so I loaned you $50. Last winter you wanted a new coat. You didn't like your blue coat. You said that young people don't wear blue coats. You needed a white coat, so I loaned you $150; then you wanted to buy a pair of pants. I gave you $15 and you bought that extremely ugly pair of pants—green with one orange spot. Yesterday you told me that your coat was dirty. Even though I was very busy, I brought it to the store for cleaning which cost $11. You owe me $226. Please pay me tomorrow.

■ EXERCISE IV

Sign the following sentences to your students. Have each student take turns adding information until a story is generated.

_____t_____
PARTY, I LOVE. YESTERDAY NIGHT, I GO-TO PARTY WITH MY FRIEND. ARRIVE. ENTER. AWFUL HAPPEN!

(I love parties. Last night I went to a party with my friend. We got there, went in, and the most awful thing happened!)

■ EXERCISE V

Pick two students in the class to sign Dialogue 6 on page 203
of *A Basic Course in American Sign Language.* To test
comprehension, ask the class to answer the following
questions:

1. What do young people have now that older deaf people did
   not have?

2. When did Don first buy a TTY? How much did it cost?

3. How have TTY's changed?

4. Why is it important to have a TTY?

5. Compare the past with the present. Which is better?

130

■ *NOTES*

LESSON 20

Conditional Sentences

Conditional sentences have two parts: *the condition* and *the consequence.* The sentences are made by:
1. Raising the eyebrows during the *condition* (represented by ____ if ____, and lowering them during the consequence.
2. Optionally the *condition* may be preceded by either SUPPOSE or #IF.

■ SET I
Practice Sentences

```
           if
```
1. TEACHER GONE, GO ROOM 103.

```
               if
```
2. #IF YOU GO COLLEGE NTID, I GO GALLAUDET.

```
        if
```
3. YOU DRIVE, PUT-IN-GAS.

```
                 if
```
4. #IF I I-GIVE-YOU MY TELEPHONE NUMBER,
```
        q              q
```
   YOU TO-TELEPHONE? PROMISE?

```
      if          n           if/n
```
5.   STUDY, TEST NOT DIFFICULT. NOT STUDY,
   DIFFICULT.

```
             if
```
6. SUPPOSE I I-GIVE-YOU $5.00,
```
              q
```
   YOU BUY TICKET FOR ME?

```
              if
```
7. SUPPOSE EAT CANDY, COOKIES, BECOME FAT WILL.

$$\overline{\qquad\qquad\text{if}\qquad\qquad}\quad\overline{\qquad\text{q}\qquad}$$
8. SUPPOSE EAT CANDY, COOKIES, BECOME FAT?

$$\overline{\qquad\qquad\text{if}\qquad\qquad}$$
9. I OUTSIDE. PAT TO-TELEPHONE, YOU-SUMMON-ME.

$$\overline{\qquad\qquad\text{if}\qquad\qquad}$$
10. #IF YOU JOIN FOOTBALL TEAM,

$$\overline{\qquad\qquad\text{q}\qquad\qquad}$$
YOU HAVE TIME STUDY YOU?

$$\overline{\qquad\text{if}\qquad}\quad\overline{\text{whq}}$$
11. SUPPOSE ROOM EMPTY, WHAT-TO-DO?

$$\overline{\qquad\qquad\text{if}\qquad\qquad}$$
12. #IF SET-UP GOAL, WORK (with attention), YOU SUCCEED CAN YOU.

$$\overline{\qquad\text{if}\qquad}$$
13. SUPPOSE I ANGRY, I SUPPRESS.

$$\overline{\qquad\text{if}\qquad}\quad\overline{\qquad\text{y}\qquad}$$
14. #IF USE GUN STEAL, WILL GO JAIL 3-YEAR WILL.

■ *NOTES*

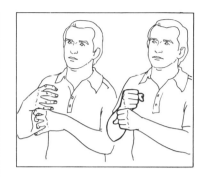

Conditional Sentences

Conditional sentences have two parts: *the condition* and *the consequence.* The sentences are made by:
1. Raising the eyebrows during the *condition* (represented by _____ if _____, and lowering them during the consequence.
2. Optionally the *condition* may be preceded by either SUPPOSE or #IF.

■ Set II
Practice Sentences

        ‾‾‾‾‾‾if‾‾‾‾‾‾
1. ANSWER RIGHT, WIN $1,000.

    ‾‾‾‾if‾‾‾‾ ‾‾‾‾n‾‾‾‾
2. #IF YOU LAZY, SUCCEED NEVER.

       ‾‾‾‾‾if‾‾‾‾‾
3. SUPPOSE GO JAIL,

‾‾‾‾‾‾‾‾‾‾‾q‾‾‾‾‾‾‾‾‾‾‾
GOVERNMENT SUBTRACT RIGHT VOTE?

     ‾‾‾‾if‾‾‾‾
4. #IF GO JAIL, GOVERNMENT SUBTRACT RIGHT VOTE.

    ‾‾‾‾‾if‾‾‾‾‾ ‾‾‾‾n‾‾‾‾
5. #IF YOU SEND MY LETTER, NOT FORGET STAMP.

   ‾‾‾‾if/n‾‾‾‾ ‾‾whq‾‾
6. SUPPOSE NOT VOTE, HAPPEN?

    ‾‾‾‾‾if‾‾‾‾‾ ‾‾‾whq‾‾‾
7. #IF YOU RETIRE, ALL-DAY WHAT-TO-DO?

    ‾‾‾‾if‾‾‾‾ ‾‾y‾‾
8. WORK (carelessly), FIRE WILL.

9. $\overline{\text{#IF MEAT SMELL BAD, THROW-AWAY.}}^{\text{if}}$

10. $\overline{\text{MR. JACKSON LECTURE, BORING.}}^{\text{if}}$
$\overline{\text{MR. JOHNSON LECTURE, INTERESTING.}}^{\text{if}}$

11. $\overline{\text{#IF MARTY NOT TO-TELEPHONE, I SAD.}}^{\text{if/n}}$

12. $\overline{\text{#IF READ CHAPTER SUMMARY,}}^{\text{if}}$
$\overline{\text{YOU UNDERSTAND MY LECTURE WILL.}}^{\text{y}}$

13. $\overline{\text{I RETIRE AGE 62, GOVERNMENT IT-PAY-ME \$20,000}}^{\text{if}}$
$\overline{\text{ANNUALLY. I RETIRE AGE 65, IT-PAY-ME \$25,000}}^{\text{if}}$
ANNUALLY.

14. I RECENTLY BUY PICTURE. I THINK VALUABLE MAYBE.
$\overline{\text{#IF VALUABLE, I SAVE. FUTURE I I-GIVE-HER}}^{\text{if}}$
DAUGHTER.

■ *NOTES*

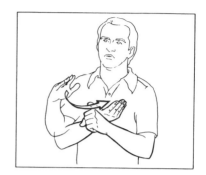

Rhetorical Questions

WH-question signs can be used as rhetorical questions to draw attention to additional information which the signer will provide. However, rhetorical questions differ from ordinary WH-questions in that the eyebrows are raised instead of squeezed together. ____ rq ____ indicates raised eyebrows for the rhetorical question.

■ SET I

Practice Sentences

```
              n              rq
```
1. I DON'T-LIKE FRANK. WHY? HE LIE-REPEATEDLY.

```
                rq
```
2. PRETTY SUNRISE. WHERE? M-O-N-T-A-N-A.

```
            rq
```
3. I SUCCEED. HOW? STUDY (with attention) ASK-
   REPEATEDLY. (with attention)

```
            rq
```
4. MEETING. WHEN? TIME 6.

```
            rq
```
5. I BUY TV NEW. WHICH? R-O-Y-A-L.

```
            rq
```
6. TEACHER FIRED. WHO? MISS SMITH.

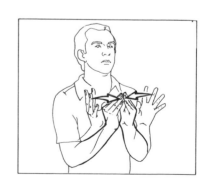

7. I DECREASE 15 POUNDS.
```
   rq                          n
```
   HOW? EAT NONE BREAKFAST, NONE LUNCH.

```
            rq
```
8. I, #JOB NEW. WHERE? PHILADELPHIA!

```
            rq
```
9. I ANGRY. WHY? SOMEONE STOLE MY TROPHY
   BASKETBALL.

Rhetorical Questions

WH-question signs can be used as rhetorical questions to draw attention to additional information which the signer will provide. However, rhetorical questions differ from ordinary WH-questions in that the eyebrows are raised instead of squeezed together. ___ rq ___ indicates raised eyebrows for the rhetorical question.

■ **SET II**

Practice Sentences

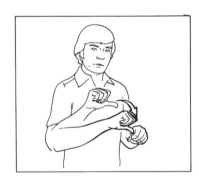

1.
$$\overline{\text{BASKETBALL C-O-A-C-H NOT HE-PICK-ME.}}^{\text{n}} \quad \overline{\text{WHY?}}^{\text{rq}} \text{ I}$$
SHORT.

2. I WRONG-REPEATEDLY. $\overline{\text{WHY?}}^{\text{rq}}$ $\overline{\text{I NOT STUDY.}}^{\text{n}}$

3. I SAVE GAS. $\overline{\text{HOW?}}^{\text{rq}}$ RIDE B-U-S.

4. PRESIDENT PICK WOMAN V.P. $\overline{\text{WHO?}}^{\text{rq}}$ ANNE CROSS.

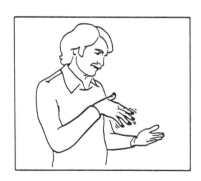

5. MY PARENTS FINALLY DECIDE FLY-HERE. $\overline{\text{WHEN?}}^{\text{rq}}$ IN-2-WEEK.

6. NEXT-YEAR MEETING. $\overline{\text{WHERE?}}^{\text{rq}}$ L.A.

7. J-U-R-Y DECIDE FINISH. $\overline{\text{WHICH?}}^{\text{rq}}$ GUILTY.

8. I POSTPONE GO-TO DENTIST. $\overline{\text{WHY?}}^{\text{rq}}$ I VERY-AFRAID.

9. KEN RECENTLY VACATION. $\overline{\text{WHERE?}}^{\text{rq}}$ F-L-A.

Exercises

■ EXERCISE I

Sign two to three sentences. . . .

1. in which one sentence uses the sign *"HOW"* as a rhetorical.

2. in which one sentence uses the sign *"HOW"* to ask a question.

3. in which one sentence includes the sign *"VERY-ROUGH"*.

4. in which one sentence includes the sign *"FRUSTRATED"-REPEATEDLY* with an appropriate facial expression.

5. in which one sentence includes the sign *"5-WEEK-AGO"*.

6. in which one sentence includes the sign *"FRUSTRATED"* as a conjunction with an appropriate facial expression.

7. in which one sentence uses the classifier *"CL:3"* to show motion.

8. in which one sentence makes a noun plural by adding a number.

9. with an agonized facial expression in which one sentence includes the sign *"HURT"-CONTINUALLY*.

10. in which one sentence starts, $\overline{\quad\textit{if}\quad}$ *"SUPPOSE. . ."*

11. with a worried facial expression in which one sentence starts, *"YOURSELF. . ."*.

12. in which one sentence includes the sign *"THAT-ONE"*.

13. in which one sentence commands someone to do something.

14. in which one sentence includes the signs *"TIME 4"*.

15. in which one sentence uses the sign *"FINISH"* to show that the action has been completed.

■ LESSON 20

Exercises

16. in which one sentence starts, "#IF. . . . "
$$\overline{if}$$

17. in which one sentence uses the sign "WHY" as a rhetorical.

■ EXERCISE II

Complete the following sentences:

                $\overline{if}$

1. #IF I ARRIVE LATE,

                $\overline{if}$

2. POTATO TASTE BAD,

                $\overline{if}$

3. SUPPOSE MIRROR BREAK,

                $\overline{if}$

4. #IF RUN-OUT-OF PAPER,

                $\overline{if}$

5. #IF YOU WASTE MONEY,

                $\overline{if}$

6. SUPPOSE WE WIN GAME TODAY,

                $\overline{if}$

7. #IF CANDY VERY-SOUR,

                $\overline{if}$

8. ROB WORK-CONTINUALLY 3-HOUR,

                $\overline{if}$

9. I BECOME ACT-AGENT FAMOUS,

                $\overline{if}$

10. #IF YOU FAIL TEST,

Exercises

■ EXERCISE III

Complete the following sentences using the rhetorical indicated in the parentheses:

1. PRESIDENT LECTURE FINISH; AUDIENCE APPLAUD _____ .
   (why)

2. I ARRIVE VERY-EARLY _____ . (why)

3. YESTERDAY MY GOOD-FRIEND AND HER BOYFRIEND
   GO PERFORMANCE. TICKET COST _____ .
   (how-much)

4. BICYCLE RACE _____ . (when)

5. I DON'T-WANT LIVE CALIFORNIA _____ . (why)

6. I FINALLY PASS DRIVE-AGENT TEST _____ .
   (how)

7. LIBRARY CLOSE _____ . (when)

8. MY SISTER GO COLLEGE _____ . (where)

9. COMMITTEE IT-PICK-HER _____ . (who)

10. POLICEMAN GIVE-TICKET ME _____ . (why)

11. NEXT-YEAR I TRAVEL-TO PUERTO-RICO _____ .
    (how)

12. FIX MY SON HIS HEARING-AID _____ .
    (how-much)

13. DANCE _____ . (where)

        t
    _____
14. MY PURSE, STEAL _____ . (how)

15. I GROW-UP _____ . (where)

16. LAST-YEAR I TRAVEL _____ . (where)

■ *NOTES*

LESSON 21

Quantifiers: Pluralizing Classifiers

Pronominal classifiers can be reduplicated to form plurals.

Classifier:1 Incorporating Number

The classifier CL:1 is used to show direction of movement of an upright human or animal. Note that the palm side of the CL:1 classifier represents the front of the human or animal.

Other Uses of Classifier:1

The classifier CL:1 can use different movements to show actions of upright humans or animals.

■ SET I
Practice Sentences

1. MY PARENTS GO-AWAY VACATION. I HAVE CL:ĽĽ DIRTY CL:BB. TOMORROW THEY ARRIVE HOME. TONIGHT MUST WASH-DISH.

2. YESTERDAY I WANT SEE MOVIE. ARRIVE. CL:44 (long line).

<u>   t   </u>
3. TEACHER CL:1, STUDENT CL:1(4)-GO-UP-TO-TEACHER.

4. I JEALOUS. DOROTHY VERY-THIN. DAILY HER CL:ĽĽ HAVE FOOD CL:B.

<u>   t   </u>
5. RIVER, BOY CL:1(2)-GO-UP-TO-RIVER.

<u>   t   </u>
6. CLOTHES WASH-IN-MACHINE, IMPORTANT HAVE 2 CL:BB (right), CL:BB (left) SEPARATE. (Point right) CLOTHES COLOR, (point left) WHITE.

■■■■ **LESSON 21**

Quantifiers: Pluralizing Classifiers

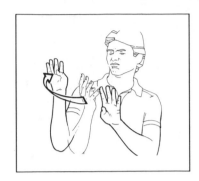

$$\overline{\quad\quad\quad\quad\text{t}\quad\quad\quad\quad}$$
7. THAT HOUSE, FRONT, HAVE BICYCLE CL:Å-ALL-OVER.

$$\overline{\quad\quad\quad\quad\text{t}\quad\quad\quad\quad}$$
8. TEACH SIGN LANGUAGE,
$$\overline{\quad\quad\quad\quad\text{t}\quad\quad\quad\quad}\quad\quad\overline{\quad\text{t}\quad}$$
 CHAIR CL-V̈-IN-A-SEMI-CIRCLE (right) CL-V̈-IN-A-ROW
(left), (semi-circle) BETTER.

$$\overline{\quad\text{t}\quad}\quad\overline{\quad\quad\quad\text{if}\quad\quad\quad}$$
9. BEER, PERSON DRINK-REPEATEDLY, OFTEN CL:1-
STAGGER. (carelessly)

10. POLICEMAN CL:1(2)-COME-RAPIDLY-UP-TO-ME. THEY
THEY-BAWL-OUT-ME.

11. DESK HAVE PAPER CL:B-ALL-OVER.

$$\overline{\quad\quad\quad\quad\quad\text{t}\quad\quad\quad\quad\quad}$$
12. PEOPLE WANT BUY TICKET L-O-T-T-E-R-Y, WOW, CL:44
(long line).

$$\overline{\quad\quad\quad\quad\quad\quad\text{n}\quad\quad}$$
13. I WANT PAPER CL:B-IN-A-ROW, NOT CL:B-ALL-OVER.
$$\overline{\quad\quad\quad\quad\text{n}\quad\quad\quad}$$
14. I DON'T-LIKE THAT AIRPORT. HAVE AIRPLANE CL:Y-ALL-
OVER. I PREFER CL:Y-IN-A-ROW.

■ *NOTES*

Quantifiers: Pluralizing Classifiers

Quantifiers Pluralizing Classifiers

Pronominal classifiers can be reduplicated to form plurals.

Classifier:1 Incorporating Number

The classifier CL:1 is used to show direction of movement of
an upright human or animal. Note that the palm side of the
CL:1 classifier represents the front of the human or animal.

Other Uses of Classifier:1

The classifier CL:1 can use different movements to show
actions of upright humans or animals.

■ SET II
Practice Sentences

1. CLOTHES CL:B-ALL-OVER.

2. TODAY WORK BUSY! BOSS CL:1-COME-UP-TO-ME-
   REPEATEDLY.

3. THAT STREET HAVE MANY RESTAURANT CL:Å-IN-A-
   ROW.

       ‾‾t‾‾
4. FATHER CL:1, BOY SMALL CL:1-WALK-UP-TO-FATHER-
   SLOWLY.

5. THAT CITY UGLY. HAVE BUILDING CL:Å-ALL-OVER.

6. MY MOTHER CL:1-COME-UP-TO-ME.

                        ‾‾whq‾‾
7. THERE CHILDREN CL:V̈-IN-A-ROW. WHAT'S-UP?

8. MY BROTHER WASTE FOOD. HE HAVE CL:L̈L̈, FOOD
   CL:B. EAT FINISH, LEFT CL:B-SLIGHTLY-SMALLER.

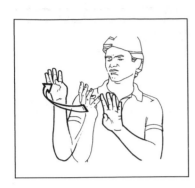

9. DOG CL:V̈-IN-A-ROW. $\overline{\text{WHY?}}$ DOG CONTEST.
    rq

10. NEAR WINDOW I HAVE PLANT CL:C-IN-A-ROW. GROW
    BEST THERE.

11. TOMORROW NEED CLOTHES WASH-IN-MACHINE. HAVE
    DIRTY CLOTHES CL:BB.

12. MY BOYFRIEND, I CL:1(2)-WALK-ALONG. MY DOG CL:V̈-
    WALK-ALONG-BEHIND-US. FOLLOW.

13. N.Y. HAVE BUILDING TALL CL:Å-ALL-OVER.

14. LOOK-AT. ARMY-AGENT CL:∧-IN-A-ROW. VERY-CUTE
    THEY!

■ *NOTES*

■ **EXERCISE I**

Sign two to three sentences. . . .

1. in which one sentence includes the classifier "CL:Å"-IN-A-ROW.

2. in which one sentence starts, "$\overline{SUPPOSE}^{if}$ . . . ".

3. in which one sentence includes the sign "KNOW"

    preceded by a topicalized clause: $\overline{}^{t}$, ... know.

4. in which one sentence includes the classifier "CL:1(3)".

5. with a shocked facial expression in which one sentence includes the sign "VERY-FAST".

6. with a careless facial expression in which one sentence includes the sign "DRIVE-TO".

7. in which one sentence includes the sign "SEE~NONE".

8. in which one sentence includes the sign "STAY"-CONTINUALLY with a facial expression showing "WITH EASE".

9. in which one sentence compares flying with driving.

10. with a determined facial expression in which one sentence includes the modal "MUST".

11. in which one sentence starts, "HERSELF . . . ".

12. in which one sentence includes the sign "I-GIVE-CL:C ↑ - HER".

13. in which one sentence uses the sign "WHERE" as a rhetorical.

14. in which one sentence is made negative without using the sign "NOT".

15. in which one sentence asks a negative yes/no question.

16. in which one sentence shows a condition without using the sign *"#IF"* or *"SUPPOSE"* (——$\overset{if}{}$——, ...).

17. in which one sentence is in the *"OBJECT + SUBJECT + VERB"* word order.

18. in which one sentence includes a verb incorporating direction.

19. in which one sentence includes the sign *"HERE"*.

20. in which one sentence includes the classifier *"CL:B"*.

■ EXERCISE II

Translate the following paragraph into American Sign Language, then sign it to your partner. When you are finished, ask your partner five questions based on the story.

(Hint: Remember, if you are comparing two things, you should set one of them up on your right and the other on your left. You can then refer to them by pointing to the proper location.)

    I want to go to college. Last fall I applied to NTID and Gallaudet. Three weeks ago, I got a letter from NTID. NTID accepted me! Today I got a letter from Gallaudet. Gallaudet accepted me! I can't decide which one I want to go to. I want to become either a teacher or a photographer. If I decide to become a teacher, I must go to Gallaudet; I can't go to NTID. Gallaudet is a four-year school; NTID is a two-year school. But, I think . . . . four years of school! That's a long time! Maybe I would prefer a two-year school. I enjoy taking pictures very much—and in two years I would be finished and could get a job and earn money. But, when I see a group of children, I look at them, and I really feel like I'd prefer teaching. I don't know what to do. I must think about it long and hard. It is a very important decision.

■ EXERCISE III

After studying the following sentences, sign them as quickly as possible using the facial expression indicated in the parentheses. Have your partner copy exactly what you have signed, including your facial expression.

1. I FEEL VERY-SICK. (Sick)

2. MY TEAM VERY-LOUSY, WE LOSE-REPEATEDLY. (Disgusted)

3. SIGN VERY-SLOW, PLEASE. (Imploring)

4. $\overline{\quad\quad t \quad\quad}$ $\overline{\quad nq \quad}$
   BACKPACKING, NOT DIFFICULT? (Unsure, Questioning)

5. $\overline{\quad t \quad}$
   HAMMER, YESTERDAY I LOST. (Disgusted)

6. $\overline{\quad t \quad}$ $\overline{\quad q \quad}$
   CANDY, VERY-SOUR? (Suspicious, Questioning)

7. $\overline{\quad\quad\quad n \quad\quad\quad}$
   I ENJOY TRAVEL. (Pleasant) I DON'T-LIKE STAY HOME. (Very Negative)

8. MY FATHER LAY-OFF. NOW MONEY DIFFICULT. (Sad)

■ *NOTES*

LESSON 22

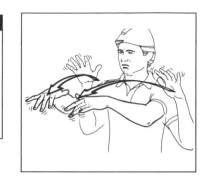

Classifiers Showing Motion

Some classifiers can be used to show the motion of the humans, animals, or objects they represent.

■ SET I

Practice Sentences

1. YESTERDAY NIGHT MY SON LEFT WATER CL:4↓. TODAY I I-BAWL-OUT-HIM.

2. STUDENT, THEY GO FACTORY, LOOK-AT NEWSPAPER CL:44⇒.

3. LUNCH ROOM SET-UP. HOW? PEOPLE CL:∧-IN-A-ROW, $\overline{\text{rq}}$ over HOW?
   FOOD CL:44⇒.

4. $\overline{\text{t}}$ over first part, $\overline{\text{t}}$ PEOPLE LIVE NORTH U.S., WINTER, CL:55↕↕ SOUTH.

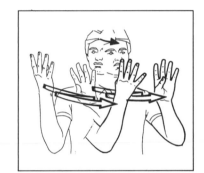

5. $\overline{\text{t}}$ AIRPORT, PEOPLE CL:∧-IN-A-ROW, LOOK-AT SUITCASE++ CL:44⇒.

6. 2-WEEK-AGO DEAD BODY LIE-DOWN THERE, PEOPLE CL:44⇒.

7. BEFORE MONDAY I LECTURE 2-HOUR. I VERY-NERVOUS, CL:4↓-FROM-FOREHEAD-CONTINUALLY.

8. $\overline{\text{t}}$ $\overline{\text{rq}}$ NIGHT, HORSE CL:55↕↕ B-A-R-N. WHY? EAT.

9. $\overline{\text{if}}$ #IF MY FINGER (point to finger)
   $\overline{\text{if}}$ $\overline{\text{q}}$ BLEED CL:4↓-CONTINUALLY 7-HOUR, I DIE?

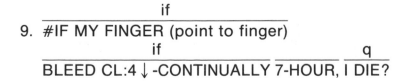

Classifiers Showing Motion

Some classifiers can be used to show the motion of the humans, animals, or objects they represent.

■ SET II

Practice Sentences

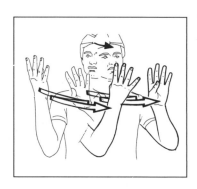

1. 3-MONTH BEFORE NEW MEXICAN RESTAURANT OPEN. PEOPLE CL:55 ⚡ ⚡ .

2. TEACHER OPEN-DOOR, CHILDREN CL:44⇒.

3. $\overline{\qquad\qquad\text{if}\qquad\qquad}$
SUPPOSE I LEFT WATER CL:4↓-CONTINUALLY 6-HOUR,
$\overline{\quad\text{whq}\quad}$
HAPPEN WHAT?

4. ALL-NIGHT BEER CL:CC CL:4↓. ENTER ROOM, SMELL VERY-BEER!

5. DOG CL:44⇒. JUDGE CRITICIZE-EACH-OF-THEM.

6. RESTAURANT VERY-NICE. HAVE FISH DIFFERENT++ CL:44⇒. STAND LOOK-AT-EACH-OF-THEM, PICK FAVORITE.

7. THAT BOY NOSE-CL:4↓-CONTINUALLY. $\overline{\quad\text{q}\quad}$ HE SICK?

8. YOUR CUP HAVE H-O-L-E CL:F. COFFEE CL:4↓.

9. PRETTY WOMAN CONTEST, WOMAN CL:44⇒. ALL VERY-BEAUTIFUL.

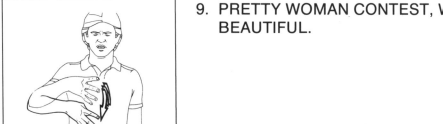

■ EXERCISE I

Sign two to three sentences . . . .

1. in which one sentence includes the sign *"OPPOSE"* and uses the *"OBJECT + SUBJECT + VERB"* word order.

2. with a frightened facial expression in which one sentence includes the sign *"BUG"*.

3. in which one sentence asks a yes/no question.

4. in which one sentence includes the classifier *"CL.Ч"-IN-A-ROW*.

5. with a contented facial expression in which one sentence includes the classifier *"CL:CC"*.

6. in which one sentence commands someone to do something.

7. in the past tense with a bored facial expression.

8. in which one sentence uses the subject as a topic.

9. with an embarrassed facial expression in which one sentence includes the sign *"I-TAKE-ADVANTAGE-HER"*.

10. with a confused facial expression in which one sentence includes the modal *"SHOULD"*.

11. in which one sentence starts, *"YOURSELF . . . "*.

12. in which one sentence shows a plural by reduplicating the sign.

13. with a disappointed facial expression in which one sentence includes the sign *"25¢"*.

14. in which one sentence includes the sign *"YOU-INFORM-ALL-OF-THEM"*.

15. in which one sentence makes a comparison.

◼ *NOTES*

16. in which one sentence starts *"#IF . . ."*.

17. in which one sentence is a rhetorical question using the sign *"WHERE"*.

18. in which one sentence includes the classifier *"CL:Å"-ALL-OVER*.

19. with a sophisticated facial expression in which one sentence includes the classifier *"CL:1"* to show movement.

20. in which one sentence includes the quantifier *"CL:B"*.

◼ EXERCISE II

Translate the following story into ASL and sign it to your partner. When you are finished, ask your partner five questions based on this story.

   For class, I had to write an explanation about the meaning of a picture. The picture was all white with one blue circle in the middle. I looked at that picture again and again, but still I didn't understand it. I asked my friend to help me. He is good at drawing, so I thought maybe he would understand this picture. He stared at it for an hour. I waited and waited. Finally, he looked at me. I felt sure he understood it. But he just shrugged his shoulders. I was disappointed. I don't know what to do. Do you know what a white picture with a blue circle in the middle means?

◼ EXERCISE III

Sign the following sentences to your students. Have each student take turns adding information until a story is generated.

<u>   t   </u>
STREET, I WALK CL:1. HAPPEN, NOTICE MAN CL:1 (following me) CLOSE. I I-LOOK-AT-HIM MAN. HE VERY-STRANGE. HE . . .

(I was walking down the street when I noticed a man following behind me. I looked at the man. He was really strange! He . . . .)

■ EXERCISE IV

Pick two students in the class to sign Dialogue 7 on
page 233 of *A Basic Course in American Sign Language.*
To test comprehension, ask the class to answer the
following questions:

1. What did Jack get?

2. When?

3. How does he feel about it?

4. What does it look like?

5. How does it work?

■ EXERCISE V

Sign a short paragraph explaining your feelings about ASL.

■ *NOTES*

APPENDIX I

■ NUMBER PRACTICE

3	21	926	2,242	24
6	79	638	7,014	4
2	16	167	8,221	210
9	84	396	7,666	647
0	230	836	2,736	412
15	790	196	9,968	835
25	666	648	8,367	953
85	238	207	6,657	795
23	354	537	2,265	111
13	826	487	8,286	493
65	921	452	2,444	917
90	124	169	8,012	614
33	275	486	7	316
58	532	864	11	169
84	865	400	14	532
12	789	555	48	142
54	520	467	2	231
57	185	631	97	121
74	308	298	8	965
38	953	2,387	30	837
69	175	8,238	10	729
88	709	3,834	60	379
93	900	3,987	21	634
45	437	1,578	89	282
70	725	6,900	5	425
96	915	9,765	65	113
57	200	4,275	47	577
38	835	1,253	64	491
75	111	7,025	75	744
64	423	7,966	18	366
83	525	3,699	1	590
39	700	7,878	35	958
69	103	5,515	19	305
26	777	8,023	85	827
62	425	3,010	63	218
98	739	1,111	28	346
79	628	2,654	54	150
60	197	8,520	22	613
44	478	5,837	57	927
84	783	6,325	37	340
24	534	2,089	59	875
40	312	8,896	17	937
29	675	7,278	16	190
30	100	8,367	3	1,122

Number Practice

3,709	22,113	28,449	788,825	185,990
2,313	27,740	19,703	841,355	471,879
7,815	86,356	67,611	321,356	634,351
8,673	40,528	23,835	452,477	772,723
4,237	21,861	70,555	235,668	563,133
1,601	38,233	59,277	532,115	948,655
4,725	50,946	36,195	123,721	1,228,565
3,456	13,630	92,414	344,232	4,478,533
6,925	22,118	44,591	251,345	5,212,589
6,748	66,364	83,884	130,113	5,953,144
5,580	47,566	50,504	261,213	8,164,943
9,988	94,523	35,623	788,440	2,549,650
7,102	47,566	42,886	291,392	3,862,877
4,375	94,523	50,933	587,095	8,853,190
1,231	74,728	63,777	352,968	7,727,463
9,621	30,311	12,080	426,814	9,643,821
8,490	85,170	23,198	777,666	1,798,322
9,203	58,215	80,322	454,730	2,255,441
5,611	46,592	75,644	938,571	9,617,915
2,513	99,148	56,425	344,775	1,346,670
6,033	97,390	34,363	505,623	3,653,324
4,415	51,815	80,067	290,015	5,486,513
6,033	40,289	11,128	313,981	4,519,199
1,820	32,488	62,446	889,801	6,396,489
1,119	72,923	29,112	621,180	7,278,858
9,780	64,284	76,330	840,201	8,238,774
1,201	83,422	32,273	155,872	7,315,433
2,016	25,055	62,614	133,960	8,492,177
3,314	70,430	50,226	764,053	9,436,365
1,725	67,149	27,965	786,716	6,175,968
2,496	16,231	17,827	692,140	1,093,361
4,333	18,111	31,708	717,233	3,424,472
13,011	69,544	48,907	909,099	6,562,811
67,546	36,660	90,758	320,576	8,777,635
36,612	77,731	56,170	540,621	9,855,956
51,743	80,475	22,810	351,113	8,659,849
74,519	25,817	88,692	873,545	2,187,560
16,265	50,152	17,522	962,925	4,133,010
28,054	43,524	62,343	284,062	4,521,427
79,323	64,699	21,430	898,179	6,823,108
85,984	31,100	72,560	295,498	7,912,393
46,139	42,438	219,941	516,200	7,594,149
13,112	58,523	402,220	327,333	0,351,716
24,897	19,838	551,662	818,833	4,628,433
31,624	21,232	464,873	929,423	7,980,152
69,270	95,908	192,315	297,157	9,176,836
15,782	27,699	267,711	366,361	1,290,299

 **NUMBERS**

zero

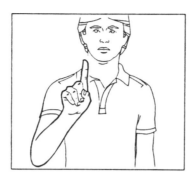

one

two

three

four

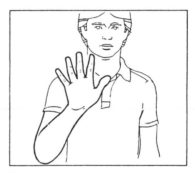

five

six

seven

eight

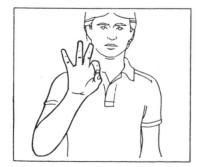

nine

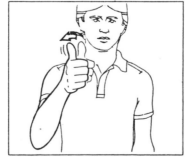

ten

eleven

twelve

thirteen

fourteen

fifteen

sixteen

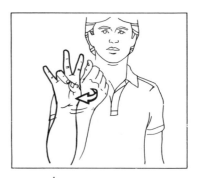

seventeen

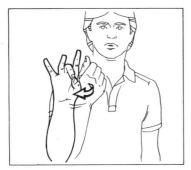

eighteen

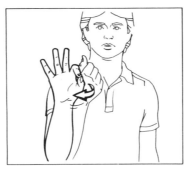

nineteen

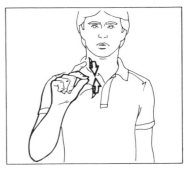

twenty

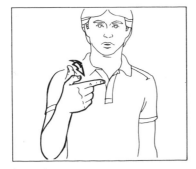

twenty-one

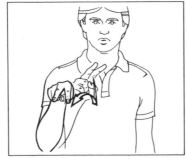

twenty-two

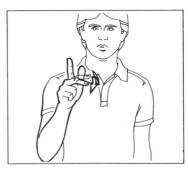

twenty-three

Numbers

twenty-four

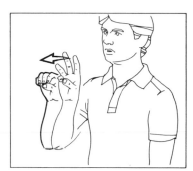
twenty-five

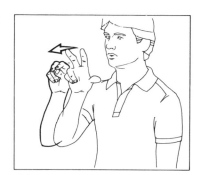
thirty

forty

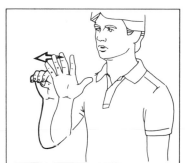
fifty

sixty

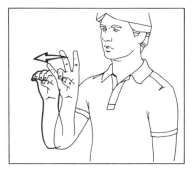
seventy

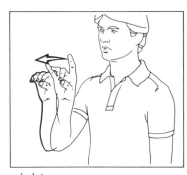
eighty

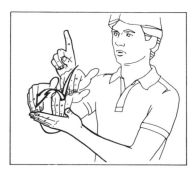
ninety

one hundred

one thousand

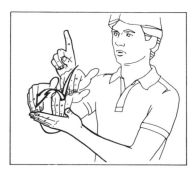
one million

APPENDIX II

■ MIME ACTIVITIES

The instructor should take the initiative in demonstrating typical miming situations and establish a pattern of practice activity for the students. The instructor may also encourage the students to devise situations of their own creation for additional practice.

1. Skiing down a hill
2. A dog taking care of its pups
3. Dressed up for the night while changing a flat tire
4. Giving out candy for Halloween
5. Watching a football game on TV, drinking a beer, and eating popcorn as the team alternately does well and badly
6. Parachuting
7. Policeman giving someone a ticket
8. Changing into a monster
9. A little boy's first day at T-ball
10. A day at the amusement park
11. Gearing up for a football game
12. Waking up late and getting into a traffic jam on the day of an important early morning meeting
13. A rock singer
14. A dog in a dog show
15. A little girl trying to lie to her mother
16. Going on a blind date
17. Watching a scary movie
18. Having a dental appointment when one is terrified of the dentist
19. A race horse
20. A boy asking a girl out for a date for the first time
21. The night before Christmas and Christmas morning
22. A chicken

APPENDIX III

■ ANSWER KEY

LESSON 1. Basic Sentence Structure: Sentences with
Predicate Adjectives

■ **SET I**

1. John is strong.
2. Kathy is angry.
3. You are short.
4. You are pretty.
5. You are interesting.
6. She is beautiful.
7. Jackie is deaf.
8. They are tired.
9. Jennifer is mad.
10. Paula is hard-of-hearing.

■ **SET II**

1. I'm hard-of-hearing.
2. Paul is tired.
3. Linda is dumb.
4. Lois is sleepy.
5. I'm deaf.
6. You are pretty.
7. Bobby is strong.
8. They are happy.
9. You are short.
10. They are hearing.

LESSON 2. Basic Sentence Structure: Sentences with
Identifying Nouns and Using Two Third-Person
Pronouns

■ **SET I**

1. She is her mother.
2. She is her friend.
3. She is her niece.
4. He is her student.
5. Your teacher is a man. He is my grandfather.
6. John is hard-of-hearing. Judy is deaf. He is her teacher.
7. Louie is my friend. Pat is his uncle. Pat is his teacher.
   Pat is smart. Louie is dumb.
8. My student, Lori, is deaf. She is pretty. My student, Gloria,
   is deaf. She is ugly. Lori is Gloria's aunt.

■ **SET II**

1. He is her father.
2. She is her grandmother.
3. She is her teacher.
4. She is her aunt.
5. Lisa is deaf. Her grandfather is hearing. Her grandmother
   is hard-of-hearing. Her parents are deaf.
6. Paula is my friend. Her friend, Kathy, is pretty. Kathy is
   hard-of-hearing.

7. My aunt is deaf. She is a teacher. My friend, Frank, is her student. He is hearing.
8. My mother is short. My father is tall. I'm short. My mother is deaf. My father is hard-of-hearing. I'm deaf.

LESSON 3. Basic Sentence Structure: Pronouns and Nouns

■ SET I

1. The girl likes me.
2. My father is a cook.
3. John knows my sister.
4. My uncle knows your name.
5. Your father remembers my mother.
6. Paula forgot the paper.
7. Your mother lost the book.
8. My wife has paper.
9. My husband needs a car.
10. My aunt is a teacher.

■ SET II

1. Your teacher wants a book.
2. My aunt wants money.
3. His wife is a student.
4. My daughter practices sign.
5. My brother likes cars.
6. Your mother remembers my car.
7. The woman needs a chair.
8. My friend needs a car.
9. My student has paper.
10. My friend is a dancer.

LESSON 3. Basic Sentence Structure: Adjectives and Nouns

■ SET I

1. Paul likes pretty women.
2. Mother wants blue paper.
3. I have a new bed.
4. I know a short woman.
5. His sister lost the red box.

6. I have a new house.
7. My niece likes blue cars.
8. I need to practice the new signs.
9. I know the old man.
10. I found a black chair.

■ SET II

1. Louie found the orange book.
2. I want to talk with the old man.
3. My class wants a new book.
4. My mother has a yellow chair.
5. I enjoy learning new signs.
6. I remember the old woman.
7. My brother has green paper.
8. Jack found a white package.
9. Your grandmother has a beautiful desk.
10. I like the new book.

LESSON 4. Negatives

■ SET I

1. John doesn't want blue paper.
2. Jean doesn't want a new table.
3. She isn't my sister.
4. I don't like fingerspelling.
5. I'm not surprised.
6. Lisa doesn't understand the movie.
7. The cat isn't expensive.
8. The food doesn't taste good.

■ SET II

1. I don't see your teacher.
2. Mrs. Smith isn't my aunt.
3. I don't like practicing.
4. She doesn't want a yellow table.
5. Jack didn't lose the paper.
6. Fran isn't an American.
7. Joan isn't short.
8. The sentence isn't wrong.

▉▉ APPENDIX III

Answer Key

Lesson 4. Responses to Yes/No Questions

▪ SET I

English Translation	Possible ASL Answer
	$\overline{\quad\quad\text{y}\quad\quad}$
1. Do you learn vocabulary?	YES, I LEARN.
	$\overline{\quad\quad\text{y}\quad\quad}$
2. Is the desk white?	YES, IT WHITE.
	$\overline{\quad\quad\text{y}\quad\quad}$
3. Do you prefer a heavy car?	I PREFER.
	$\overline{\quad\quad\text{y}\quad\quad}$
4. Do you need a new book?	I NEED.
	$\overline{\quad\quad\quad\text{y}\quad}$
5. Is the book interesting?	YES, IT INTERESTING.
	$\overline{\quad\quad\text{y}\quad\quad}$
6. Isn't the table heavy?	YES, IT HEAVY.
	$\overline{\quad\quad\text{y}\quad\quad}$
7. Don't you enjoy reading?	YES, I ENJOY.
	$\overline{\quad\quad\quad\text{y}\quad}$
8. Your father isn't hearing?	YES, HE HEARING.

▪ SET II

English Translation	Possible ASL Answer
	$\overline{\quad\quad\text{y}\quad\quad}$
1. Do you enjoy class?	YES, I ENJOY.
	$\overline{\quad\quad\text{y}\quad\quad}$
2. Do you believe me?	I BELIEVE.
	$\overline{\quad\quad\text{y}\quad\quad}$
3. Is your good friend sick?	YES, HE SICK.
	$\overline{\quad\quad\text{y}\quad\quad}$
4. Do you need a small box?	I NEED.
	$\overline{\quad\quad\quad\text{y}\quad}$
5. Is the car expensive?	YES, IT EXPENSIVE.
	$\overline{\quad\quad\text{y}\quad\quad}$
6. Don't you love me?	YES, I LOVE YOU.

7. She doesn't want an orange?
$$\overline{\text{YES, SHE}}^{\text{y}}\text{ WANT.}$$

8. You're not reading Exercise 5?
$$\overline{\text{YES, I}}^{\text{y}}\text{ READ.}$$

Lesson 4. Responses to Negative Questions

▪ SET I

English Translation	Possible ASL Answer
1. Does his grandmother like cats?	$\overline{\text{NO, SHE DON'T-LIKE.}}^{\text{n}}$
2. Is your house old?	$\overline{\text{IT NOT OLD.}}^{\text{n}}$
3. Do you know Marcie Smith?	$\overline{\text{NO, I DON'T-KNOW.}}^{\text{n}}$
4. Is your aunt eating your orange?	$\overline{\text{NO, SHE NOT EAT.}}^{\text{n}}$
5. Does she need blue paper?	$\overline{\text{SHE NOT NEED.}}^{\text{n}}$
6. Don't you like to cook?	$\overline{\text{NO, I DON'T-LIKE.}}^{\text{n}}$
7. You're not angry?	$\overline{\text{NO, I NOT ANGRY.}}^{\text{n}}$

▪ SET II

1. Do your parents like dogs?	$\overline{\text{THEY DON'T-LIKE.}}^{\text{n}}$
2. Do you understand the lesson?	$\overline{\text{I NOT UNDERSTAND.}}^{\text{n}}$
3. Do you remember the name of the movie?	$\overline{\text{I NOT REMEMBER.}}^{\text{n}}$
4. Does your niece enjoy dancing?	$\overline{\text{NO, SHE NOT ENJOY.}}^{\text{n}}$
5. Does your family like your husband?	$\overline{\text{THEY DON'T-LIKE.}}^{\text{n}}$
6. Isn't your table new?	$\overline{\text{NO, IT NOT NEW.}}^{\text{n}}$
7. He doesn't want to teach?	$\overline{\text{NO, HE DON'T-WANT.}}^{\text{n}}$

■ APPENDIX III

Answer Key

LESSON 5. Basic Sentence Structure:
Present, Past, Future, and Using FINISH

■ SET I

1. A long time ago he liked to work.   Now he doesn't like to work.
2. Yesterday it was cold.
3. Did they already find the small box?
4. Tomorrow my sister will buy a cookie.
5. In the future I will visit Washington.
6. Later I will practice signing.
7. Did Sarah already buy a TTY?
8. I used to practice signing. Now I don't.
9. John already telephoned Jack.
10. I wrote the letter.

■ SET II

1. My brother felt sick yesterday.   Today he's improved.
2. Recently I went to Washington.
3. Last night grandmother died.
4. In the future I will buy a new car.
5. My sister recently found a dog.
6. I wrote the sentence.
7. I will buy paper later.
8. Paul already bought the book.
9. I remembered your name yesterday.   Now I don't remember it.
10. I'm finished working.

LESSON 6. Basic Sentence Structure:
Object + Subject + Verb

■ SET I

1. My sister already saw the movie.
2. I'm practicing signing.
3. My family needs a car.
4. My deaf friend doesn't like the public school.
5. Does your uncle enjoy reading?
6. My son doesn't like green pants.
7. My friend, Kathy, needs an umbrella.
8. The teacher lost my book.

9. My sister wants money.
10. Did your daughter already buy the bicycle?

■ **SET II**

1. I like to dance.
2. My mother doesn't know sign language.
3. I've visited Washington.
4. Paul's daughter lost my bicycle.
5. I've already written the letter.
6. My sister bought a new watch.
7. My aunt wants an umbrella.
8. Sally visited grandfather.
9. I finished reading the book.
10. I didn't like the movie.

LESSON 6. Directional and Non-Directional Verbs

■ **SET I**

1. I showed mother my picture yesterday. She said it was pretty.
2. I'm shy. YOU ask her.
3. Will you give me an orange, please?
4. Did you give me the money?
5. Will you ask her to buy me a new book?
6. The teacher asked ME; she didn't ask YOU!
7. Pauly told me a funny joke.
8. I already paid you!
9. She gave her a spider plant yesterday.
10. Did you already give her the stack of pictures?

■ **SET II**

1. Did you tell me your address?
2. Did I give you the TTY?
3. I don't want mother to force me to learn to drive.
4. My brother influences me.
5. John and Karen are good friends. She gave him a cute cat last Thursday.
6. Last Friday Connie paid me. Did you pay me last Saturday?
7. I want to show you the new umbrella.
8. Did I send you my picture last Monday?
9. Did you give her the book?
10. Later she'll give you water.

■ APPENDIX III

Answer Key

LESSON 7. Imperatives and Using Numbers

■ SET I
1. Give me 3 pencils.
2. Tomorrow I'm going at 10:00.
3. I planned 2 lessons.
4. Buy 4 plants, please.
5. My brother is 30 years old.
6. Send me 4 pictures.
7. At lunch yesterday, I drank 5 cokes.
8. Class is finished at 3:15.
9. For homework, write 3 advertisements.
10. My parents eat dinner at 5:00. I prefer 6:30.

■ SET II
1. Buy 7 tickets.
2. I have 2 stamps left.
3. Order 3 hamburgers and 4 french-fries, please.
4. Yesterday I bought 4 plates.
5. I have a brother 7 years old and a sister who is 5.
6. Call me tomorrow at 4:30.
7. Yesterday my brother ate 3 hamburgers.
8. Send mother 5 plants.
9. I'm 59 years old. John asked me my age; I told him 49. He believed me!
10. Tomorrow I'll stay home until 3:00 in the afternoon.

LESSON 7. Personal Pronouns Incorporating Numbers and Plurals

■ SET I
1. Paul and John (the two of them) are 10 years old.
2. They (the five of them) are from California.
3. When class is finished, the three of you stay.
4. John and I (the two of us) are taking sign language.
5. Are the four of you 14 years old?
6. My mother has many coats.
7. Give me a few pencils, please.
8. John found several bus tickets.
9. On the fingerspelling test, I had many mistakes.
10. I'm cooking a few hamburgers.

■ **SET II**

1. Yesterday my sister and I (the two of us) visited grandmother.
2. We (the four of us) are from Ohio.
3. The three of us want water.   The three of them want milk.
4. They (the two of them) have brown eyes.
5. The five of us understand.   He doesn't understand.
6. Today several people are sick.
7. Yesterday I wrote many sentences.
8. My aunt has several cats.
9. I saw many movies.
10. Yesterday John taught me a few signs.   I enjoyed it.

LESSON 8. WH-Questions

■ **SET I**

1. How much candy do you have?
2. Where is the bathroom?
3. Why did you draw the picture?
4. Do you want ice cream or candy?
5. How do you feel? Sick?
6. How many children do you have?
7. What's your name?
8. Who's lonely? You?
9. How much food is left?
10. Why did you buy several pairs of pants?

■ **SET II**

1. Who made the cookies?
2. When did Albert become a doctor?
3. What broke?
4. Who informed you?
5. When did the child run away?   Yesterday?
6. Where do you work?
7. What did you find?
8. How many hours did you study?
9. What did you do yesterday?
10. What time is it?

APPENDIX III

Answer Key

LESSON 8. The SELF Pronoun

■ SET I

1. I cooked the hamburger yesterday.
2. How many horses did he buy?
3. We cleaned up.
4. You go with mother.
5. I want to talk to the man myself.
6. I made a mistake.
7. You send the man the advertisement.
8. Don't YOU ask him. I want to ask him myself.
9. Does she have 3 coats?
10. I'll inform you.

■ SET II

1. You ask the teacher.
2. I eat lunch at 12:00.
3. He reads many books.
4. I'm planning the party.
5. I'm sending you the letter myself.
6. How much money do you need?
7. You explain to Pat.
8. I'll force you to sign.
9. Did your daughter buy the pants herself?
10. My brother is 7 years old.

LESSON 9. Noun-Verb Pairs

■ SET I

1. Jack, put on your hearing aid!
2. My hearing aid broke.
3. Where is the comb?
4. Do you like rain?
5. It is raining today.
6. Cinderella is my favorite story.
7. Jackie is good at telling stories.
8. Did you wash the window?
9. Open the window.
10. Buy the book, *A Basic Course in American Sign Language*

▪ SET II

1. Open the book to page 6.
2. Where do you work?
3. I worked last Monday.
4. Did you buy the ring?
5. Call me tomorrow night at 6:00.
6. Yesterday my sister bought a new telephone . . . it's blue.
7. Sit down!
8. Yesterday was my niece's birthday.   I gave her a ring.
9. John put the ring on Judy's finger.
10. Do you favor the Redskins?

LESSON 10. Basic Sentence Structure: Using Modals and Negative Modals

▪ SET I

1. Can you send her the box tomorrow?
2. Can the two of us go to the beach?
3. I refuse to get up at 5:00 in the morning!
4. Grandfather has already visited Cleveland.
5. Tomorrow I *WILL* study for one hour.
6. You should leave at 6:15.
7. You must give me the stamp tomorrow!
8. I've already typed the homework.
9. Your friend hasn't shown up yet.
10. Maybe John and I will get married.

▪ SET II

1. I can ride a bicycle.
2. You must send her a letter.
3. I've finished planning the party.
4. You must practice signing!
5. Tomorrow she *WILL* give you the umbrella!
6. She didn't see the performance yet?
7. The meeting isn't set up yet.
8. I can't take sign language.
9. I *WILL* pass the driving test.
10. You must memorize the "Gettysburg Address."

■■ APPENDIX III

LESSON 11. Verbs Incorporating Location and Using FINISH as a Conjunction

■ **SET I**

1. I drove from home to S.F., then I drove to L.A. from S.F. I left my car in L.A. and flew home.
2. I walked to the store, bought food, then walked home.
3. I recently brought 5 books to school.   2 were stolen; 3 are left.
4. My friend's house is close to school.   When she was young, she walked to school and back home again.
5. I live in N.J. and work in N.Y.   In the morning, I drive to N.Y.; in the afternoon, I drive to N.J. (from N.Y.)
6. I'll go to the library and study, then I'll come home and eat.
7. I'll work for one hour, then I'll go to the movies.
8. I'll explain it to Mary, then she'll explain it to you.
9. I'll tell a story, then you go to sleep. O.K.?
10. I'll lecture for a few minutes, then you'll take the test.

■ **SET II**

1. I want to bicycle from Chicago to N.Y.
2. I'll read the book, then I'll come to your house.
3. I cook dinner, clean up, then eat.
4. Yesterday my sister, brother, and I ate at the restaurant over there, then we went to the football game.
5. I'll give you the telephone number, then you call.
6. I'll move to S.F., wait one week, then try to find a job.
7. Last summer I drove to my sister's house, visited for a week, then flew to Fla.   My parents live there.
8. Tomorrow I'm driving to the residential school.   I have a meeting with my son's teacher.
9. Last Saturday my friend got married.   I drove to my boyfriend's house, then the two of us drove to the church.
10. I urge you to go to the meeting.

LESSON 12. Locational Relationships and Adding Movement to Pronominal Classifiers

SET I

1. My car is next to your car.
2. The van is behind the blue car.
3. A man is standing behind a woman.
4. A child is standing on a table.
5. My cup is next to the paper.
6. A leaf is under the tree.
7. I followed the bus in my car.
8. My car was parked over there, and a bus came right up behind it and bumped it.
9. Do you see the car over there and the boy standing next to it? He's cute.
10. I was sitting reading a book. I got up and walked to the refrigerator.

SET II

1. Did you park behind my car?
2. The boy standing next to the car, is that Jeff?
3. The glass is next to the book.
4. I want the blue glass behind the plate.
5. My bed and my sister's bed are at right angles to each other.
6. Open the door that is next to the table.
7. Ben is standing next to the window.
8. The glass was lying on its side on the table. I picked it up and righted it.
9. My friend is mad. He was standing under a tree. I walked up to him. He turned around and walked away.
10. Over there is a beautiful green and red kite flying above.

LESSON 13. Mass Quantifiers

SET I

1. I must read a book that is this thick. (CL:G)
2. The desk has 2 stacks of papers on it. (CL:BB ↑ ↓, CL:BB ↑ ↓)
3. Today I got this many letters. (CL:L̈)

4. Some people arrive early.
5. I'm eating a little bit of pie.
6. The President's car has thick windows! (CL:G)
7. I'll buy dinner. I have plenty of money.
8. I have to grade a large stack of papers. (CL:Ḷ)
9. My friend brought some magazines yesterday.

■ **SET II**

1. There is a stack of books on the shelf. (CL:BB ↑ ↓)
2. The sign language book is this thick! Wow! (CL:Ḷ)
3. I made a cookie that was this big and this thick. (CL:ḶḶ, CL:G)
4. Come to my house and eat. I have plenty of food.
5. I practiced my lecture a little bit.
6. There was this much cream on this much milk. (CL:G, CL:Ḷ)
7. The bookstore has a fingerspelling book that is this thick. (CL:Ḷ) Is that the one I should buy?
8. Some men prefer tall women.
9. My notebook is this thick! (CL:Ḷ)
10. My son knows a little sign language.

LESSON 14. Negatives; Negative Quantifiers

■ **SET I**

1. John doesn't want any help.
2. I don't see any paper.
3. I don't eat vegetables at all.
4. My sister recently moved. Her furniture hasn't arrived yet. She has no furniture.
5. I never depend on my parents.
6. I've never seen a blue cookie.
7. That monkey is lazy. He's not playing at all.
8. My father heard a noise in the basement. I didn't hear anything.
9. I never memorize dates for tests.
10. Yesterday my dog died. I haven't felt anything.
11. That teacher never plans her lessons.
12. In 20 minutes we're going to leave. You haven't packed a thing!
13. Last Friday I didn't have any homework.
14. My sister never obeys the rules.
15. My parents have no patience.

■ **SET II**

1. I don't have any boyfriends.
2. My aunt decided herself. There wasn't any discussion.
3. I was hammering and hit my finger with the hammer. I felt nothing. I was surprised.
4. I didn't hear that John Glenn wanted to become President.
5. My friend never washes the car.
6. Sue isn't satisfied at all.
7. I've never tried smoking.
8. I haven't seen TV for a long time.
9. The restaurant doesn't have any hamburgers.
10. I've waited since 3 o'clock for the man to announce the race. . . .There hasn't been one.
11. Did you understand the lecture? I didn't understand it at all.
12. All day I haven't eaten a thing. Now I have a headache.
13. I never practice typing.
14. My dog never chases cats.
15. I don't have any money.

LESSON 14. Use of NOTHING

■ **SET I**

1. I didn't sell your cat!
2. Last Friday I didn't go with your boyfriend!
3. I didn't challenge you to a bicycle race!
4. I didn't eat your candy!
5. I didn't shave the dog's head!

■ **SET II**

1. I didn't steal the money!
2. My father doesn't wear a dress!
3. I didn't force Judy to lie!
4. I didn't break your wristwatch!
5. I'm not bothering you!

LESSON 15. Directional Verbs

■ **SET I**

1. You put down a sentence. I'll copy you.
2. Tomorrow there is a Sadie Hawkins dance. Can I borrow your blue dress and black shoes?

3. The committee picked me to lecture.
4. Last Monday I took a test. Joe copied from me.
5. Do you think Fred wants to take me to the party?
6. Last month I tried to join a baseball team, but they didn't pick me.

■ **SET II**

1. When you're finished working, call me. The two of us will go to the beach.
2. Yesterday I was sick. Can I copy your notes? Thank you.
3. Last month you borrowed my hammer. This month you borrowed my screwdriver. Now you want to borrow my wrench? You're taking advantage of me.
4. Chuck, Ed, Tony and I felt that the lecture was boring. The three of them picked me to tell the speaker.
5. When dinner is ready, call me.
6. Will you take me to the dance?

LESSON 15. Directional Verbs Incorporating Two Objects

■ **SET I**

1. I will arrive at 6:00 in the morning. Tell both of them.
2. I've already asked both of them.
3. The two of them washed my car yesterday. I gave both of them five dollars.
4. That man chose you and me? What for?
5. I will force both of them to use sign.

■ **SET II**

1. Jane picked both of them to become the leaders.
2. I want to show both of you.
3. I sent both of them my picture already.
4. I'll give the two of you a coke and the two of you a beer.
5. I borrowed money from both of them. I took advantage of them.

LESSON 15. Directional Verbs Incorporating EACH or ALL

■ **SET I**

1. The teacher asked each of you.
2. Did I already show all of you my engagement ring?
3. The game was cancelled because of rain.   Did I tell all of you?
4. Tomorrow I'll decide.   I'll let you all know.
5. This afternoon I'll pay each of you three dollars.
6. I'll let each of you know my decision tomorrow.
7. I suggested we leave tomorrow.   They all told me they'd prefer to leave tonight.

■ **SET II**

1. When school is over, I'll let each of you know your grade.
2. I've already told all of you, you *must* arrive at 10:00.
3. I want to show all of you my shirt from California.
4. Yesterday I told all of you, you *must* come on time.
5. Last Saturday I loaned each of you three dollars.
6. You borrow from each of us—stop it!
7. None of you studied.   I'm going to give all of you more homework.

LESSON 16. Time Measurements and Tense Indicators
            Incorporating Number

■ **SET I**

1. For the last 6 months I've worked as a teacher.   I enjoy it.
2. Last year my sister moved to Fla.   Next summer I'll drive there and visit.   I'll stay 2 weeks then drive home.
3. Last week did you tell me your name?
4. Three years ago my boyfriend and I were walking and saw a car accident.
5. I've been sick for the last 8 weeks.   It's been difficult to study.
6. Two weeks ago I bought a backpack.
7. In 6 months I going to get married.
8. Four years ago I graduated from college.
9. For the last 3 years I haven't gotten a raise.   I'm disappointed.
10. You continue playing for 5 minutes then go to sleep.

■ SET II

1. I waited 2 hours for the bus.   Finally it came.   I was angry. I bawled out the bus driver.   He didn't care.
2. To earn enough money to buy that coat, I must work 3 days.
3. My baby will be born in 4 months.
4. I met your brother 3 weeks ago.   He's nice . . . friendly.
5. In 6 months I'm going to join a deaf baseball team.
6. Two weeks ago I loaned you $5.00.
7. Tomorrow in speech class I must give a 3-minute speech. I'm nervous.
8. Today I interpreted for 3 hours.
9. I will continue working.   In 5 minutes, call me.
10. Two years ago I went by boat to Europe.

LESSON 16. Time Reduplication and Repetition

■ SET I

1. Every Thursday my sister, brother, and I eat together.   Last Thursday we ate at my house.   Next Thursday we'll eat at my sister's house; the following Thursday we'll eat at my brother's house.
2. Every year you should go to the doctor.
3. Every week I spend $50.00 for food.
4. Every Monday night I eat hamburgers.
5. Every day lunch costs $3.00.
6. Every year a mouse gets into my house.
7. Every 3 years I drive to Chicago to visit my good friend.
8. I'm taking a science class that meets from 9:00 to 11:00 every Saturday.
9. Every 3 months I get a raise called "cost of living".

■ SET II

1. Do you eat fish every Friday?
2. Every 2 years I visit Europe.
3. I want to work every Saturday.
4. Every 3 hours I must milk the cow.
5. Every week I must write 15 sentences.
6. Every day we learn new vocabulary.
7. Every 2 months Gallaudet College offers sign language classes.   I wish I could join one, but I can't.   I work.
8. Everyday at 6:00 in the morning and 6:00 at night, I take a green pill.   Every 3 hours I take an orange pill.   It's awful.
9. Every month I have a large stack of bills. (CL:L̈)

Answer Key

LESSON 17. Comparative Sentences

■ SET I

1. I prefer washing dishes to washing clothes. I don't know the reason.
2. Gallaudet is farther than NTID.
3. A headache is worse than a cold.
4. Eating at home is cheaper than eating at a restaurant.
5. Most people prefer snow to rain.
6. The new car is quieter than the old car.
7. The blue pants are smaller than the brown pants.
8. My brother is shyer than my sister.

■ SET II

1. My child is smarter than your child.
2. Exercising every 2 days is better than exercising every day.
3. Dogs are friendlier than cats.
4. My sister is nicer than my brother.
5. Randy prefers teaching to interpreting.
6. I prefer orange cars to red cars.
7. Western U.S. is dryer than Eastern U.S.
8. My suitcase is lighter than your suitcase.

LESSON 17. Conjunctions

■ SET I

1. I was reading the newspaper when out of the blue I remembered my appointment. (hit)
2. Last week I bought 6 beautiful flowers, but they all died. (frustrate)
3. For the last 6 months I hadn't called my friend. Yesterday I called and found out that she had moved to Nebraska. (find)
4. In 1932, 300 deaf people moved to Ohio. (happen)
5. I dated Joe for 5 months when I found out that he was already married. (find)
6. Paul and Mary were married for 6 months when they got divorced. (happen)
7. Last night I studied Lessons 6 and 7. Today I found out that the test was on Lessons 8 and 9, not on 6 and 7. (find)

8. Two weeks ago I went to a basketball tournament and found out that it was cancelled. I wasn't informed. (frustrate)
9. I was driving when suddenly a car came up behind me and smashed into the back of my car. (wrong)

■ **SET II**

1. This morning I went to the bank and found out that it was closed. I forgot that today is a holiday—Veterans' Day. (frustrate)
2. I was sitting outside when unexpectedly it started to rain. (hit)
3. My girlfriend and I were discussing where to bicycle. She said Gates Mills; I said Chagrin Road. At the end of the discussion we decided on Gates Mills. That was fine. When we got there, we found out that her idea of Gates Mills and my idea of Chagrin Road were the same place. (find)
4. Last year my brother died. (happen)
5. Last fall I planned to take a science class, but it was cancelled. (frustrate)
6. I was on a date with Fred when unexpectedly Mike showed up! (wrong)
7. Last June I finally found a job. I worked for 4 months when the company closed. (happen)
8. I planned to interpret a meeting when unexpectedly I got sick and couldn't go. (hit)
9. My friend and I decided to eat lunch at a famous restaurant. When we arrived, we found that it was closed. (frustrate)

■ **EXERCISE II—ASL TRANSLATION**

LAST-YEAR I EARN MONEY PLENTY, DECIDE FLY-TO CHICAGO (right). I GO-WITH GOOD-FRIEND DEBBIE. FLY-TO

$$\overline{}^{\,t}$$

CHICAGO SATURDAY MORNING. SATURDAY AFTERNOON, VISIT MY GIRLFRIEND LOUISE. SHE LIVE CHICAGO SINCE

$$\overline{}^{\,t}$$

1980. SATURDAY NIGHT, DEBBIE AND I EAT RESTAURANT NEAR L-A-K-E M-I-C-H. FOOD DELICIOUS BUT EXPENSIVE— COST $63.00 FOR TWO-OF-US. WOW! EAT FINISH, GO

$$\overline{}^{\,t}$$

PERFORMANCE. FUNNY. ENJOY. SUNDAY AFTERNOON,

$$\overline{}^{\,t}$$

SHOP FINISH, B-U-S RIDE-TO AIRPORT. TIME 3 FLY-TO-HERE HOME. WE ENJOY CHICAGO. HOPE VISIT AGAIN FUTURE.

LESSON 18. Verb Inflection: -REPEATEDLY

■ SET I

1. I failed the driving test again and again. (carelessly) Finally, last month I passed.
2. Mr. Smith is a bad teacher. He doesn't explain anything. I have to repeatedly ask him questions. (with attention)
3. Complain, complain, complain, you're never satisfied.
4. When I explain to Paul, he understands. To Harry, I explain over and over and over again and still he doesn't understand. (with attention)
5. My daughter is forever losing her watch. (carelessly)
6. That man keeps looking at that woman over there. (with attention)
7. I have to take a pill for my stomach, take a pill for my head, take a pill for my back. All day, I take pills. (with effort)
8. Before, when I was young, my girlfriend and I used to go to the library all the time. (with ease)
9. My uncle is lucky. He's always finding money.
10. The reason you've learned nothing all this time is because you're absent again and again. (carelessly)
11. At the meeting, the people applauded over and over again. (with attention)
12. My father has diabetes. He has to get shots repeatedly.
13. I told my friend that I would call her on the TTY on Thursday. Thursday, I called her over and over again, but she wasn't home. (with effort)

■ SET II

1. I've loaned you money again and again totaling $60. When are you going to pay me back?
2. For the last 3 weeks I've helped you with your homework many times. (with effort) Today I don't want to help you. Sorry.
3. My grandmother and I argue all the time. (with effort)
4. I've analyzed the sentence many times, and still I don't understand it. (with attention)
5. Last week I was on vacation. This week people are calling me and calling me and calling me.
6. I told Danny again and again not to telephone me after 10:00. Last night he called at 11:15. I'm fed up. (with effort)
7. I have to repeatedly put gas in my car. (with effort)

8. I enjoy sports.   I don't know the reason.   I lose all the time. (carelessly)
9. Don't carelessly take pills.   (carelessly)   Read the bottle carefully.   (with attention)
10. I announced it again and again.   You weren't paying any attention.
11. Her daughter complains all the time.
12. For the last 2 weeks you've been bothering me all the time. Stop it!
13. I often go to my uncle's house.   (with ease)

LESSON 18. Verb Inflection:-Continually

■ SET I

1. Working all the time and not playing at all is boring. (with attention)
2. Yesterday was my birthday.   My family went to a restaurant. I ate and ate and ate.   (with ease)
3. When I was a kid, I didn't understand church.   It seemed that you stood continually for nothing.
4. Every Saturday morning my sister continually looks at TV. (with ease)
5. For graduation, I interpreted continually.   (with attention) When it was finished, my feet hurt.
6. I analyzed and analyzed the picture.   (with attention)
7. Every morning that girl combs her hair continually for one hour! (with attention)
8. My father promised to come visit my daughter.   She waited and waited.   (with ease)   He didn't show up.   She cried for some time.   I felt sorry for her.
9. I enjoy visiting my sister.   I stay for two hours.   (with ease)
10. Paula is a good worker.   She works continually all day. (with attention)
11. I hate dating.   I meet a man.   I give him my telephone number and I wait and wait and wait for him to call.
12. I went to the doctor's and sat for a long time.   Finally the doctor was ready.
13. For the last 2 weeks, my head has hurt continually.
14. That teacher is awful.   He's talked continually for three hours! (carelessly)
15. Last night I struggled for a long time with my homework. (with effort)

■ **SET II**

1. I don't exercise at all. I sit all day long. (with ease)
2. I'm dieting. I don't eat breakfast or lunch, and that's fine. But at night, I eat continually. (carelessly)
3. That man with the green eyes and blond hair is staring at you. (with attention) I've never met him. Do you know his name?
4. I've been hammering continually for a long time with no success. (with attention)
5. That woman smokes continually. (carelessly)
6. Interpreting using the Rochester Method means to fingerspell continually. (with attention) Many deaf people don't like it. They say that continually watching fingerspelling is boring and their eyes get tired.
7. Yesterday John told me a joke. I laughed and laughed and laughed.
8. For the last three hours, I've worked continually. (with attention)
9. I'm hungry. When school is finished, I'll hurry home and eat and eat and eat.
10. Yesterday morning I stayed in bed for a long time. (with ease) I got up at 11.
11. I prefer driving to riding a bus. To ride the bus, you have to get-up early, walk there, and wait for a long time. (with effort)
12. When I visit my aunt, I stay for a long time. (with ease)
13. I waited a long time for the bus. (with effort) Finally, it arrived.
14. I work continually for 1 hour, rest for 15 minutes, work continually for 1 hour, rest for 15 minutes. (with attention)
15. For 2 hours I interpreted. (with attention)

LESSON 19. Adjective Modulation: Very-

■ **SET I**

1. I feel very sick. I think I have the flu.
2. My friend is buying a house for $13,000—very cheap.
3. Many people want to move to Arizona. Not me. It's very dry. I prefer the Eastern U.S.
4. For the last four months I've been dieting—eating 1,200 calories a day. I'm very hungry.
5. My teacher is very strict. She's always bawling me out.
6. The people living in Appalachia are very poor.

7. Your 16 year old sister is getting married next week? She's very young!
8. My aunt and uncle recently moved to Fla. Three weeks ago I drove there to visit. It was very hot! I'd *never* move there.
9. My neighbor recently moved away. Now I have a new neighbor. He's very loud. It's awful.
10. Larry's sister has a Siberian Husky. It's very white.

■ **SET II**

1. You decided to go to the doctor? Very good!
2. Three years ago I took a bus to Chicago. It was awful. The bus was very dirty and not comfortable.
3. My boyfriend is very cute. He has jet black hair and very green eyes.
4. Lisa told me a joke; it was very funny!
5. I'm very angry.
6. Sometimes I sign very fast. Sorry.
7. My sister refused to lend me her bicycle. She's very selfish.
8. That candy is very sour.
9. I bought 4 dresses, 3 pairs of pants, and 5 shirts. Now I'm very broke.
10. My boyfriend watches football game after football game. It's so boring!

LESSON 19. Adjective Modulation: -REPEATEDLY

■ **SET I**

1. My ex-boyfriend would become angry all the time. I didn't like that.
2. My niece is mischievous often.
3. I worry a lot. I'm going to get an ulcer.
4. I try to force you to sign and not talk. Still you talk and talk and talk. I get frustrated all the time.
5. My sister and brother are always late. You can't depend on them.
6. You never pay attention to your work. You're always careless and always wrong.
7. Everyday a different room. Today 105, yesterday 106, tomorrow 107. I'm fed-up!
8. Before I lived in Fla. I was hot all the time. I couldn't bear it. I decided to move to Ohio. It's better.

SET II

1. When my daughter became 18-years-old, she arrived home late again and again. I worried and worried and worried.
2. Last Monday, I called my father. He was sick with a cold. He's sick all the time.
3. The doors on the left are blue.
4. In the winter, I'm cold all the time.
5. For the last five months my uncle has been late for work repeatedly. Yesterday, he was fired.
6. Did you make alot of mistakes on the test?
7. My teacher gave me my spelling test. I looked at the test. I had many errors.
8. My child is afraid repeatedly.

LESSON 19. Adjective Modulation: -Continually

SET I

1. My girlfriend moved to Korea last year. Since then she's been sick continually.
2. That teacher is mad all the time. I don't think she likes children.
3. For the last 2 weeks my arm has hurt continually. Tomorrow I'm going to the doctor. I hope he gives me a pill.
4. Yesterday my niece and nephew came to visit. They were mischievous the whole time. I was relieved when my sister arrived.
5. Last week my boyfriend was mad for the whole week. I don't know the reason. I think there was trouble at work.
6. My vacation was terrible. I was sick the whole time.
7. I have a migraine. My head hurt all day.

SET II

1. Since May I've been sick continually.
2. When you drive to N.Y., be careful the whole time.
3. Some deaf people think lip reading is continually frustrating.
4. For a long time I've been sick. I found out that I have mononucleosis. I have to stay home for 3 weeks.
5. In science class, I want to give-up. I'm continually frustrated.

6. Before I lived in New York City.   I was continually afraid. I moved.   Now I live in N.J. It's better.
7. I've struggled for a long time with problem 7.

■ **EXERCISE III—ASL TRANSLATION**

<u>   t   </u>
MONEY, YOU OWE ME. BEFORE FALL YOU WANT BUY WATCH NEW. I I-LOAN-YOU-$50. BEFORE WINTER YOU
<u>   n   </u>
WANT COAT NEW. YOU DON'T-LIKE YOUR COAT BLUE. YOU
<u>   t   </u>   <u>   n   </u>
SAY, PEOPLE YOUNG, WEAR COAT BLUE NOT. YOU NEED COAT WHITE. I I-LOAN-YOU $150; FINISH, YOU WANT BUY PANTS. I I-GIVE-YOU $15--YOU BUY PANTS VERY-UGLY-GREEN WITH ONE CL:F ORANGE SPOT. AWFUL! YESTERDAY YOU YOU-TELL-ME YOUR COAT DIRTY. EVEN-THOUGH I
<u>   t   </u>
VERY-BUSY, YOUR COAT I BRING-TO STORE FOR CLEAN-UP. COST $11. YOU OWE ME $226. PLEASE YOU- PAY-ME TOMORROW.

LESSON 20. Conditional Sentences

■ **SET I**

1. If the teacher is gone, go to room 103.
2. If you go to college at NTID, I'm going to Gallaudet.
3. If you drive, put gas in the car.
4. If I give you my telephone number, will you call?   You promise?
5. If you study, the test won't be difficult.   If you don't study, it will be difficult.
6. If I give you $5.00, will you buy a ticket for me?
7. If I eat candy and cookies, I will get fat.
8. If I eat candy and cookies, will I get fat?
9. I'll be outside.   If Pat calls, call me.
10. If you join the football team, will you have time to study?
11. If the room is empty, what should I do?
12. If you set-up a goal and work hard, you can succeed.
13. If I'm angry, I suppress it.
14. If you use a gun to steal, you will go to jail for 3 years.

■ **SET II**

1. If the answer is right, you win $1,000.
2. If you are lazy, you'll never succeed.
3. If you go to jail, will the government take away your right to vote?
4. If you go to jail, the government will take away your right to vote.
5. If you mail my letter, don't forget a stamp.
6. If you don't vote, what will happen?
7. If you retire, what will you do all day?
8. If you work carelessly, you will get fired.
9. If the meat smells bad, throw it away.
10. If Mr. Jackson lectures, it's boring. If Mr. Johnson lectures, it's interesting.
11. If Marty doesn't call me, I'll be sad.
12. If you read the chapter summary, you will understand my lecture.
13. If I retire at 62, the government will pay me $20,000 a year. If I retire at 65, it will pay me $25,000 a year.
14. I recently bought a picture. I think it might be valuable. If it is valuable, I'll save it. In the future, I'll give it to my daughter.

LESSON 20. Rhetorical Questions

■ **SET I**

1. I don't like Frank because he lies all the time.   (Why)
2. Montana has pretty sunrises. (Where)
3. I succeed by studying hard and asking a lot of questions. (How)
4. The meeting is at 6:00.   (When)
5. I bought a new TV—a Royal.   (Which)
6. A teacher was fired—Miss Smith.   (Who)
7. I lost 15 pounds by not eating breakfast and not eating lunch. (How)
8. I got a new job—in Philadelphia.   (Where)
9. I'm angry.   Someone stole my basketball trophy.   (Why)

■ **SET II**

1. The basketball coach didn't pick me because I'm short. (Why)
2. I'm wrong again and again because I don't study.   (Why)
3. I save gas by riding the bus.   (How)

4. The President picked a woman V.P.—Anne Cross.   (Who)
5. My parents finally decided to fly here; they're coming in two weeks.   (When)
6. Next year the meeting will be in L.A.   (Where)
7. The jury decided—guilty.   (Which)
8. I postpone going to the dentist because I'm terrified.   (Why)
9. Ken recently went on vacation to Florida.   (Where)

LESSON 21. Quantifiers: Pluralizing Classifiers; Classifier: 1 Incorporating Number; Other Uses of Classifier: 1

▰ SET I

1. My parents are on vacation.   I have a pile of dirty dishes. Tomorrow they're coming home.   Tonight I have to do the dishes.
2. I wanted to see a movie yesterday.   When I got there, there was a long line of people.
3. Four students went up to the teacher.
4. I'm jealous.   Dorothy is very thin.   Everyday she has a pile of food on her plate.
5. Two boys went up to the river.
6. When you wash clothes, it's important to have 2 separate piles of clothes, 1 pile of colored clothes, the other, white.
7. In the front of that house there are bicycles scattered all over the place.
8. In teaching sign language, it's better to have the chairs in a semi-circle than in a row.
9. If a person drinks beer after beer after beer, often he will stagger.
10. Two policemen came charging up to me and bawled me out.
11. The desk has papers all over it.
12. There was a long line of people wanting to buy lottery tickets.
13. I want the papers in a row not scattered all over.
14. I don't like that airport.   There are airplanes scattered all over the place.   I prefer to have the airplanes lined up in a row.

▰ SET II

1. There are clothes scattered all over.
2. Today I was busy at work! The boss came up to me again and again.

3. That street has many restaurants lining the street (in a row).
4. The small boy walked slowly up to his father.
5. That city is ugly. It has buildings set up all over the place.
6. My mother came up to me.
7. Over there, there are children sitting in a row. What's up?
8. My brother wastes food. He has a plate full of food. After he's eaten there is still a pile of food left on his plate.
9. There are dogs lined up in a row because there is a dog show.
10. Near the window I have plants lined in a row. They grow best there.
11. Tomorrow I need to wash clothes. I have a pile of dirty clothes.
12. My boyfriend and I were walking along. My dog was walking along behind us following us.
13. N.Y. has tall buildings all over.
14. Look. There are soldiers standing in a row. They're cute!

■ EXERCISE II—ASL TRANSLATION

I WANT GO COLLEGE. BEFORE FALL I APPLY NTID (right), GALLAUDET (point left). 3-WEEK-AGO, I GET LETTER FROM NTID. IT (point right) ACCEPT ME. TODAY I GET LETTER

$$\overline{\text{FROM GALLAUDET. IT (point left) ACCEPT ME! WHICH GO,}}^{\text{rq}}$$

$$\overline{\text{I CAN'T DECIDE.}}^{\text{n}} \text{ I WANT BECOME EITHER TEACHER O-R}$$

$$\text{PHOTOGRAPH-AGENT. \#IF I DECIDE BECOME TEACHER, I}^{\text{if}}$$

$$\text{GO-TO (left) GALLAUDET MUST; } \overline{\text{CAN'T GO-TO}}^{\text{n}} \text{ (right) NTID.}$$
GALLAUDET 4-YEAR SCHOOL. NTID 2-YEAR. BUT, I THINK . . . SCHOOL 4-YEAR CONTINUE! LONG TIME! MAYBE PREFER 2-YEAR SCHOOL. I VERY-ENJOY TAKE-PICTURE—AND FINISH IN-2-YEAR, GET #JOB, EARN MONEY. BUT, HAPPEN SEE GROUP CHILDREN, I I-LOOK-AT-CONTINUALLY, FEEL LIKE I

$$\overline{\text{PREFER TEACH. WHAT-TO-DO, DON'T KNOW.}}^{\text{rq}\qquad\text{n}} \text{ I THINK-}$$
CONTINUALLLY MUST. DECISION IMPORTANT.

■ APPENDIX III

LESSON 22. Classifiers Showing Motion

■ SET I

1. Last night my son left the water running.   Today I bawled him out.
2. The students went to the plant and watched the newspapers go past on the conveyor belt.
3. The lunch room is set up with the people standing in a line and the food moving past them on a conveyor belt.
4. In the winter people living in the Northern U.S. flock to the South.
5. At the airport, the people stand in a line and watch the suitcases go past.
6. Two weeks ago there was a body laid out over there with people filing past it.
7. Last Monday I lectured for 2 hours.   I was very nervous and sweating profusely.
8. At night the horses flock to the barn to eat.
9. If my finger bleeds for 7 hours, will I die?

■ SET II

1. Three months ago a new Mexican restaurant opened up. People are flocking to it.
2. The teacher opens the door, and the children file in.
3. If I leave the water running for 6 hours, what will happen?
4. All night the beer keg was leaking.   When you walk in the room, the smell of beer is strong!
5. As the dogs file past, the judge critiques each one.
6. The restaurant is very nice.   They have different kinds of fish that move past you (on a conveyor belt).   You stand there, watch them go past, and pick your favorite.
7. That boy's nose is continually running.   Is he sick?
8. Your cup has a hole in it.   The coffee is dripping out.
9. At the beauty contest, the women file past.   They are all so beautiful!

■ **EXERCISE II—ASL TRANSLATION**

<u>   t   t   </u>
FOR CLASS, PICTURE, I MUST EXPLAIN IT MEAN, WRITE.
PICTURE (outline with index fingers ☐) ALL WHITE, 1 BLUE
CL:F, (place in the middle of the drawn ☐) MIDDLE. I I-LOOK-
<u>   n   </u>
AT-REPEATEDLY, STILL NOT UNDERSTAND. MY FRIEND
(point right), I I-ASK-HIM HE-HELP ME. HE SKILLED DRAW, I
THINK MAYBE HE UNDERSTAND THIS PICTURE. HE LOOK-
AT-CONTINUALLY ONE-HOUR. I WAIT- CONTINUALLY.
FINALLY HE HE-LOOK-AT-ME. I FEEL SURE HE
UNDERSTAND. HE "SHRUGGED HIS SHOULDERS" (mime). I
<u>   rq   n   </u>
DISAPPOINT. WHAT-TO-DO, DON'T-KNOW.
YOU KNOW MEAN PICTURE
<u>   q   </u>
WHITE OUTLINE-☐, BLUE CL:F (in the middle) MIDDLE?

■APPENDIX IV

■ THE MANUAL ALPHABET

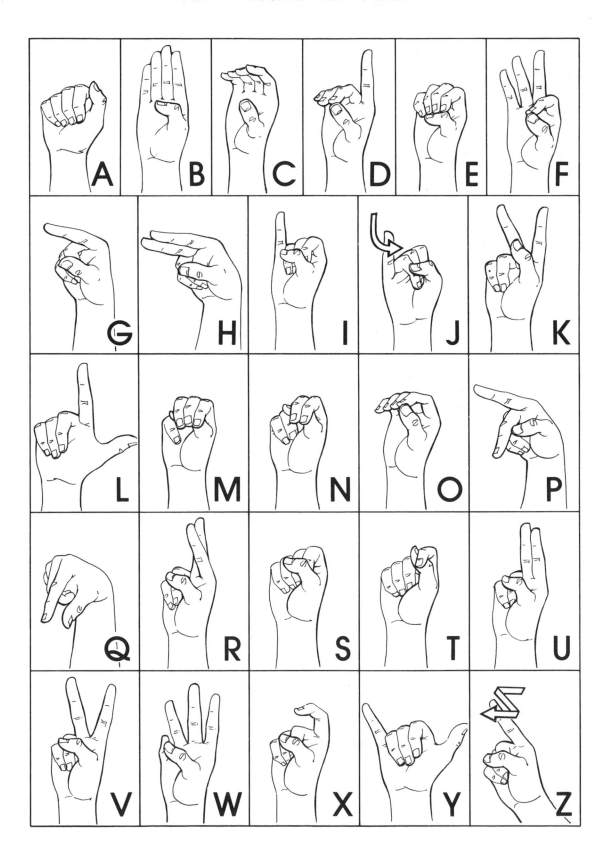

■REFERENCES

■ AMERICAN SIGN LANGUAGE

Baker, C. Regulators and Turn-taking in American Sign Language Discourse. In Friedman, L. (Ed.). *On the Other Hand: New Perspectives in American Sign Language.* New York: Academic Press. 1977.

Baker, C. and Cokely, D. *American Sign Language, A Teacher's Resource Text on Curriculum, Methods, and Evaluation.* Washington, D.C.: Gallaudet University Press. 1991.

Baker, C. and Cokely, D. *American Sign Language, A Teacher's Resource Text on Grammar and Culture.* Washington, D.C.: Gallaudet University Press. 1991.

Baker, C. and Padden, C. Focusing on the Nonmanual Components of American Sign Language. In Siple, P. (Ed.). *Understanding Language Through Sign Language Research.* New York: Academic Press. 1978.

Baker, C. and Padden, C. *American Sign Language: A Look at its History, Structure, and Community.* Silver Spring, Maryland: T.J. Publishers, Inc. 1978.

Baker, C. Sentences in American Sign Language. In Baker, C. and Battison, R. (Eds.). *Sign Language and the Deaf Community.* Silver Spring, Maryland: National Association of the Deaf. 1980.

Battison, R. *Lexical Borrowing in American Sign Language.* Silver Spring, Maryland: Linstok Press. 1978.

Battison, R. Signs Have Parts: A Simple Idea. In Baker, C. and Battison, R. (Eds.). *Sign Language and the Deaf Community.* Silver Spring, Maryland: National Association of the Deaf. 1980.

Bellugi, U. How Signs Express Complex Meanings. In Baker, C. and Battison, R. (Eds.). *Sign Language and the Deaf Community.* Silver Spring, Maryland: National Association of the Deaf. 1980.

Cogen, C. On Three Aspects of Time Expression in American Sign Language. In Friedman, L. (Ed.). *On the Other Hand: New Perspectives in American Sign Language.* New York: Academic Press. 1977.

Eastman, G., Norestsky, M. and Censoplano, S. *From Mime To Sign.* Silver Spring, Maryland: T.J. Publishers, Inc. 1989.

Fischer, S. and Gough, B. Verbs in American Sign Language. *Sign Language Studies,* 18:17–48. 1978.

Frishberg, N. Arbitrariness and Iconicity: Historical Change in American Sign Language. *Language,* 51:676–710. 1975.

Greenberg, J. *In This Sign.* New York: Holt, Rinehart and Winston. 1970.

Hoemann, H. *The American Sign Language: Lexical and Grammatical Notes With Translation Exercises.* Silver Spring, Maryland: National Association of the Deaf. 1975.

Humphries, T., Padden, C., and O'Rourke, T.J. *A Basic Course in American Sign Language, Second Edition.* Silver Spring, Maryland: T.J. Publishers, Inc. 1994.

Humphries, T., Padden, C., and O'Rourke, T.J. *Un Curso Basico De Lenguaje Americano De Senas.* Translated by Lourdes Rubio. Edited by Gilbert L. Delgado. Silver Spring, Maryland: T.J. Publishers, 1991.

Klima, E. and Bellugi, U. *The Signs of Language.* Cambridge, Massachusetts: Harvard University Press. 1979.

Lane, H. *When the Mind Hears: A History of the Deaf.* New York: Random House. 1984.

194

Lane, H. *The Deaf Experience: Classics in Language and Education.* Cambridge, Massachusetts: Harvard Press. 1984.

Liddell, S. Nonmanual Signals and Relative Clauses in American Sign Language. In Siple, P. (Ed.). *Understanding Language Through Sign Language Research.* New York: Academic Press. 1978.

Madsen, W. *Conversational Sign Language II: An Intermediate-Advanced Manual.* Washington, D.C.: Gallaudet College Press. 1972.

O'Rourke, T.J., *A Basic Vocabulary.* Introduction by Ursula Belugi. Silver Spring, Maryland: T.J. Publishers, Inc. 1978.

Smith, C., Lentz, E.M., and Mikos, K. *Signing Naturally: Student Videotext and Workbook Level I.* Berkeley, California: Dawn Sign Press. 1988.

Smith, C., Lentz, E.M., and Mikos, K. *Signing Naturally: Teacher's Curriculum Guide and Cumulative Review, Levels I & II.* Berkeley, California: Dawn Sign Press. 1988.

Spradley, T. and Spradley, J. *Deaf Like Me.* New York: Random House. 1978.

Sternberg, M. *American Sign Language—A Comprehensive Dictionary.* New York: Harper and Row. 1981.

Sternberg, M. *American Sign Language Concise Dictionary.* New York: Harper and Row. 1990.

Sternberg, M. *American Sign Language Dictionary.* New York: Harper and Row. 1987.

Stokoe, W., Casterline, D., and Croneberg, C. *A Dictionary of American Sign Language on Linguistic Principles.* Silver Spring, Maryland: Linstok Press. 1976.

Supalla, T. and Newport, E. How Many Seats in A Chair? The Derivation of Nouns and Verbs in American Sign Language. In Siple, P. (Ed.). *Understanding Language Through Sign Language Research.* New York: Academic Press. 1978.

Volterra, V. and Stokoe, W. *Sign Language Research '83; Proceedings of the III International Symposium on Sign Language Research, Rome, 1983.* Silver Spring, Maryland: Linstok Press. 1985.

Wilbur, R. *American Sign Language and Sign Systems.* Baltimore: University Park Press. 1979.

Woodward, J. and Erting, C. Synchronic Variation and Historical Change in American Sign Language. *Language Sciences.* 37:9–12. 1974.

■ DEAF COMMUNITY AND DEAF CULTURE

Bowe, F. *Changing the Rules.* Silver Spring, Maryland: T.J. Publishers, Inc. 1986.

Bullard, D. *Islay.* Silver Spring, Maryland: T.J. Publishers, Inc. 1986.

Delgado, G., editor. *The Hispanic Deaf: Issues and Bilingual Challenges for Special Education.* Washington, D.C.: Gallaudet University Press. 1984.

Gannon, J. *Deaf Heritage—A Narrative History of Deaf America.* Washington, D.C.: National Association of the Deaf. 1980.

Gannon, J., *The Week the World Heard Gallaudet.* Washington, D.C.: Gallaudet University Press. 1989.

Holcomb, M. and Wood, S. *Deaf Women: A Parade Through the Decades.* Berkeley, California: Dawn Sign Press. 1988.

Jacobs, L. *A Deaf Adult Speaks Out.* Washington, D.C.: Gallaudet College Press. 1980.

Kannapell, B. Personal Awareness and Advocacy in the Deaf Community. In Baker, C. and Battison, R. (Eds.). *Sign Language and the Deaf Community.* Silver Spring, Maryland: National Association of the Deaf. 1980.

Lane, H. *The Wild Boy of Aveyron.* Cambridge, Massachusetts: Harvard University Press. 1976.

Lane, H. Notes for A Psychohistory of American Sign Language. *The Deaf American* 30:3–7. 1977.

Meadow, K. 1972. Sociolinguistics, Sign Language, and the Deaf Subculture. In O'Rourke, T.J. (Ed.). *Psycholinguistics and Total Communication: The State of the Art.* Silver Spring, Maryland: National Association of the Deaf. 1972.

Neisser, A. *The Other Side of Silence: Sign Language and the Deaf Community in America.* Washington, D.C.: Gallaudet University Press. 1990.

Padden, C., and Humphries, T. *Deaf in America: Voices From a Culture.* Cambridge, Massachusetts: Harvard University Press. 1988.

Padden, C. and Markowicz, H. Cultural Conflicts Between Hearing and Deaf Communities. In *Proceedings of the Seventh World Congress of the World Federation of the Deaf.* Silver Spring, Maryland: National Association of the Deaf. 1976.

Padden, C. The Deaf Community and the Culture of Deaf People. In Baker, C. and Battison, R. (Eds.). *Sign Language and the Deaf Community.* Silver Spring, Maryland: National Association of the Deaf. 1980.

Sacks, O. *Seeing Voices: A Journey into the World of the Deaf.* Berkeley, California: University of California Press. 1989.

Schein, J. *At Home Among Strangers.* Washington, D.C.: Gallaudet University Press. 1989.

Stokoe, W., editor. *American Deaf Culture: An Anthology.* Silver Spring, Maryland: Linstok Press. 1989.

Stokoe, W., editor. *Sign and Culture: A Reader For Students of American Sign Language.* Silver Spring, Maryland: Linstok Press. 1985.

Van Cleve, J. and Crouch, B. *A Place of Their Own: Creating the Deaf Community in America.* Washington, D.C.: Gallaudet University Press. 1989.

Watson, D. (Ed.). *Readings on Deafness.* New York: New York University. Deafness Research and Training Center. 1973.

Woodward, J. Historical Bases of American Sign Language. In Siple, P. (Ed.). *Understanding Language Through Sign Language Research.* New York: Academic Press. 1978.

Woodward, J. Sociolinguistic Research on American Sign Language: A Historical Perspective. In Baker, C. and Battison, R. (Eds.). *Sign Language and the Deaf Community.* Silver Spring, Maryland: National Association of the Deaf. 1980.

SIGN LANGUAGE VIDEOTAPES

■ A Basic Course in American Sign Language

T.J. Publishers, 1986. A series of four tapes designed to illustrate the various exercises and dialogues in the text. Four deaf teachers and three hearing students provide a variety of models for the exercises. All tapes include voice.

VT 113A	Tape No. 1 (lessons 1–7)	(VHS)
VT 113B	Tape No. 2 (lessons 8–14)	(VHS)
VT 113C	Tape No. 3 (lessons 15–22)	(VHS)
VT 113D	Tape No. 4 Conversations	(VHS)

Tape 4 presents spontaneous, unrehearsed conversations between four Deaf adults. It provides beginning students with excellent practice in reading signs and it can be used with any sign language text. Topics discussed include:
1. mischievous behaviors of school children
2. travel experiences
3. deaf clubs
4. deaf people in different countries
5. name signs

Series Package (Includes four videotapes plus the ABC/ASL text and the Student Study Guide).

V115   (VHS)

■ A Basic Course in American Sign Language Vocabulary Videotape

T.J. Publishers, 1992. Four culturally diverse models sign each vocabulary word contained in all 22 lessons of the text plus the alphabet and numbers. The tape has captions and voice-over to enable students to utilize sound for instruction or opt to turn it off to sharpen visual acuity. Ideal for classroom reinforcement and independent home study. All featured models are Deaf and are native signers.

V325   (VHS)

■ Signs of Sexual Behavior
■ Signs of Drug Use

T.J. Publishers, 1985. These tapes are keyed to the sequence of relevant signs in the companion texts. Both the illustration number and the gloss for each sign are displayed. In addition, a side view of the signer is provided through the use of corner inserts.

| VT 103 | Signs of Sexual Behavior | (VHS) |
| VT 104 | Signs of Drug Use | (VHS) |

■ From Mime to Sign
Gilbert C. Eastman

T.J. Publishers, 1989. As a drama professor, television personality, performer and storyteller, Gil Eastman has developed a unique approach to visual communication. Now he shares his ability to combine gesture, mime, facial expression and American Sign Language in eloquent visual communication. Three videotapes correspond to the lessons in the highly illustrated text.

VT208	From Mime to Sign Video 1 Chapters 1–5	(VHS)
VT209	From Mime to Sign Video 2 Chapters 6–9	(VHS)
VT210	From Mime to Sign Video 3 Chapters 10&11	(VHS)
VT211B	From Mime to Sign Text with all Three Videos	(VHS)

■ The Parent Sign Series

This outstanding series of sign language instructional tapes has been developed and produced to present frequently used and needed vocabulary to the parents of deaf children.

Two focus families, each with a deaf and a hearing child, one with deaf parents and one with hearing parents, engage in situation-specific conversations followed by review sentences and vocabulary.

VT 131	Morning Activities at Home	VHS
VT 132	Afternoon Activities at Home	VHS
VT 133	Dinner at Home	VHS
VT 134	Evening Activities at Home	VHS
VT 135	An Afternoon at the Park	VHS
VT 136	The Fast Food Lunch	VHS
VT 137	A Birthday Party	VHS
VT 138	The Grocery Store	VHS
VT 139	Planning a Fire Escape Route	VHS
VT 140	The Dentist's Office	VHS
VT 141	Parent Sign Videotape Package 10 Tapes	VHS

All materials available from: T.J. Publishers, Inc.
817 Silver Spring Ave.
Suite 206
Silver Spring, MD 20910
1-800-999-1168

Please call or write for current order and shipping information.